THE OBERON BOOK
OF
MODERN DUOLOGUES

Chosen and Edited by Catherine Weate

OBERON BOOKS

LONDON

First published in 2009 by Oberon Books Ltd
521 Caledonian Road, London N7 9RH
Tel: 020 7607 3637 / Fax: 020 7607 3629
e-mail: info@oberonbooks.com
www.oberonbooks.com

A catalogue record for this book is available from the British Library.

ISBN: 978-1-84002-828-7

Cover photograph Stock.xchng www.sxc.hu

Printed in Great Britain by CPI Antony Rowe, Chippenham.

THE OBERON BOOK

OF

MODERN DUOLOGUES

Catherine Weate has been a voice coach for over twenty years in England, Australia, Hong Kong and India. Her work has taken her into the diverse worlds of theatre, film, radio, education, commerce, law and politics. She has been Head of Voice at Rose Bruford College, Head of Voice and Vice Principal at the Academy of Live and Recorded Arts and Head of Examinations at LAMDA. Her other publications include *The Oberon Book of Modern Monologues for Men*, *The Oberon Book of Modern Monologues for Women* and *Classic Voice*.

INTRODUCTION

Duologues are a key tool for actors, directors and teachers: the interplay between two characters over a relatively short space of time can create a dynamic challenge in rehearsals, workshops or the classroom. They're also valuable as presentation pieces. Most drama schools now rely on duologues rather than monologues for their student actors in agent showcases.

However, finding the right duologue can be a daunting task as it must stand alone outside of the context of the play it inhabits as well as meet the playing range, capabilities and needs of two actors. All of the duologues in this book have been taken from contemporary drama texts published by Oberon Books and offer up a variety of ages and cultural backgrounds in material that can be presented on its own.

There are three sections: Part One includes duologues with two female characters; Part Two presents duologues with two male characters and Part Three provides material with one male and one female character. The ages vary widely within each section, with a mix between younger and older characters, sometimes within the one scene. Duologue length also differs, from the concise and contained to the weighty and lengthy (sometimes it takes time for characters to develop and make their individual points). Although there may need to be some editing, particularly for showcase purposes, I do hope that someone somewhere will perform them complete as they were intended.

The material itself is fascinating, from the heartbreaking (*Crossfire* by Michel Azama, translated by Nigel Gearing, *The Bogus Woman* by Kay Adshead and *Cressida Among the Greeks* by David Foley) to the historical (*Get Up and Tie Your Fingers* by Ann Coburn, *Concealment* by Reza de Wet and *Under the Black Flag* by Simon Bent) to the comic (*Things You Shouldn't Say Past Midnight* by Peter Ackerman, *Love Song* by John Kolvenbach and *Mad Margaret's Revenge* by Lesley Ross). Allow these duologues to inspire you to read further and discover more about the plays they come from, not just to gain valuable insight into the characters and stories they inhabit, but for the sake of a thoroughly enjoyable read.

Catherine Weate

CONTENTS

PART ONE: FEMALE/FEMALE DUOLOGUES

PART TWO: MALE/MALE DUOLOGUES

PART THREE: FEMALE/MALE DUOLOGUES

PART ONE
FEMALE/FEMALE
DUOLOGUES

From

THE MURDERS AT ARGOS
by David Foley

Originally commissioned by the Hyperion Theatre in Seattle,
The Murders at Argos *was first performed at the New York
International Fringe Festival in August 2000.*

David Foley, an American playwright, has updated the *Oresteia*
for modern day audiences. Agamemnon returned victorious
from the Trojan war after ten years only to have his wife,
Clytemnestra, murder him in his bath. She wanted revenge for
the death of her oldest daughter, Iphigeneia, who was sacrificed
to the gods as the war ships set sail. Clytemnestra and her lover,
Aegisthus, now rule Argos together. However, Clytemnestra's
teenage daughter, ELECTRA, wants revenge for her father's death
and has sent for her brother, Orestes. In this scene we find
ELECTRA at her father's tomb, pouring libations to his spirit.
CHRYSOTHEMIS, her younger sister, runs in to warn her that
Clytemnestra and Aegisthus are on their way to the tomb.

CHRYSOTHEMIS/ELECTRA

CHRYSOTHEMIS: Electra! Electra!

ELECTRA: What is it?

CHRYSOTHEMIS: (*Breathlessly.*) I just want to tell you – that Mommy and Aegisthus are coming.

ELECTRA: Here? Why?

CHRYSOTHEMIS: To pour libations for Daddy.

ELECTRA: (*In a rage.*) Liba –? How dare they? They murdered him! How can they even think of coming here to honor his tomb?

CHRYSOTHEMIS: (*Unhappily.*) Oh, Electra! *This* is why I came! Don't, please, make a scene! Don't upset them!

ELECTRA: Don't upset *them*? Chrysothemis! What are you talking about? *They killed Daddy!* Remember? They *murdered* him.

(*Beat.*)

CHRYSOTHEMIS: (*Grudgingly.*) I know that.

ELECTRA: Well?

(*CHRYSOTHEMIS assumes the close, guarded look of someone who really resents you bringing up an uncomfortable topic.*)

CHRYSOTHEMIS: Electra, I know that Mommy and Aegisthus killed Daddy. I'm not stupid. I just don't see – frankly – what you expect me to do about it.

ELECTRA: Oh, nothing. Nothing at all. Please don't let it bother you. Forget I brought it up.

CHRYSOTHEMIS: Oh, yes, it's very easy for you! You *like* to upset people! You *like* to get them mad at you. But I have to live here – day to day.

ELECTRA: Chrysothemis! You saw the body! You saw the blood!

CHRYSOTHEMIS: Stop it! Leave me alone, Electra! You can't make me take sides!

ELECTRA: You're going to have to take sides some day. And maybe some day soon.

CHRYSOTHEMIS: What does that mean?

ELECTRA: (*With a glance at the OLD WOMAN.*) Come here. (*She pulls CHRYSOTHEMIS downstage. THE OLD WOMAN ostentatiously hums a tune and looks away to show that she isn't listening.*)

I sent for Orestes. I told him to come.

CHRYSOTHEMIS: But Mommy doesn't want Orestes back.

ELECTRA: Of course she doesn't! Because he'll kill her. She knows the minute he sets foot in Argos again she's dead.

CHRYSOTHEMIS: Oh, Electra, why can't you leave well enough alone!

ELECTRA: Well enough? Well *enough*? Oh, never mind, Chrysothemis. Go back to Mommy.

(*CHRYSOTHEMIS starts to back away, but ELECTRA grabs her roughly.*)

But listen to me, Chryssie. If you breathe a word of what I said to anyone, I'll chop you into little pieces and litter the yard with your corpse.

CHRYSOTHEMIS: (*Terrified.*) I won't! I won't! I won't!

From

BLACK CROWS
by Linda Brogan

This play was first performed at the Arcola Theatre, London, in March 2007.

Set in 1970s Manchester, *Black Crows* explores the story of three women and their love for the one man, Marionette, who is sixteen years of age (and portrayed by a puppet in the play). HAZEL is fifteen years old and mixed-race Irish/Jamaican. She is drawn to Marionette and he to her. LEONORA is thirty years old and a British-born Jamaican. She describes herself as ugly but always able to get what she wants. LEONORA gives Marionette a place to stay, food to eat and money in his pocket in exchange for time together in bed; however, now she is pregnant. HAZEL and LEONORA have already fought over Marionette in the local café. This time they meet in the supermarket and LEONORA has her mates with her. HAZEL is carrying a shopping basket when LEONORA bursts in.

LEONORA/HAZEL

LEONORA: He's mine.

HAZEL: Is he fuck.

LEONORA: He's mine.

HAZEL: Get to fuck.

LEONORA: Where was he Friday night?

HAZEL: In the gambling house.

LEONORA: All night?

HAZEL: All night.

LEONORA: In my bed.

HAZEL: You old cunt.

LEONORA: In my bed.

HAZEL: For his dinner.

LEONORA: And that's the kind of man you want?

HAZEL: Tell your mates to back off.

LEONORA: You tell 'em.

HAZEL: Tell your mates…

LEONORA: I'm telling you…

HAZEL: Tell your fucking mates to back off.

Hey, you at the fucking till, call the police.

LEONORA: Call any one you like, next time…

HAZEL: Call the fucking police.

LEONORA: Next time I won't buck you up, you won't hear me, you won't see me.

HAZEL: Why, you gonna jump under that fucking bus.

LEONORA: Little half-breed…

My man that – bought and paid for.

HAZEL: Yeah.

The ten pound you gave him bought us lunch.

Let go of me hair.

Let go of me fucking hair.

LEONORA: You might work in an office, bitch

But you ain't got no class.

Because you see your mother before you.

White women man, all man tief.

What can be expected from the mixed up daughter?

Today me go in peace – next time…

Pretty you pretty yes, but let's see what he thinks when you're nah pretty.

You understand me?

HAZEL: If your fucking mate boots me once more…

LEONORA: Kick her, Carol.

Save her face.

Me want him say he come back of his own accord.

From

A BRIEF HISTORY OF HELEN OF TROY

by Mark Schultz

This play was originally produced in the US by Soho Repertory Theater with True Love Productions Inc. and was first performed in the UK at Drum Theatre, Plymouth in September 2005.

A Brief History of Helen of Troy or *Everything will be Different* by the American playwright, Mark Schultz, explores the world of fifteen year old CHARLOTTE who is grieving over the death of her mother. She focuses on Helen of Troy for a school project and wonders if Helen's daughter, Hermione, feels the same pain and loneliness that she does. HEATHER is an imaginary friend who makes CHARLOTTE feel worthwhile. In this scene, CHARLOTTE tells HEATHER that her father has grounded her for trying to run away.

CHARLOTTE/HEATHER

CHARLOTTE: He's like obsessed.

HEATHER: He is.

CHARLOTTE: He's like really obsessed. I can't go.

HEATHER: You can't go?

CHARLOTTE: I can't go. Wherever.

HEATHER: So like he locks the door? Like he won't let you out?

CHARLOTTE: He yelled at me and he tore up my luggage.

HEATHER: What?

CHARLOTTE: He yelled at me and he tore up my luggage. He called me ugly.

HEATHER: Your dad?

CHARLOTTE: Yes.

HEATHER: You're just a little challenged is all.

CHARLOTTE: I am not ugly.

HEATHER: You are not ugly.

CHARLOTTE: I know. I want him to die. Do I have acne?

HEATHER: I don't even know what that is.

CHARLOTTE: Acne?

HEATHER: No. You don't. Wait. Yeah.

CHARLOTTE: Yes?

HEATHER: Yes.

CHARLOTTE: God. I want him to die.

HEATHER: He lets you out for school, right?

CHARLOTTE: Maybe. I don't know. It's the weekend. And I'm like grounded forever.

HEATHER: He has to let you go to school.

CHARLOTTE: I don't know. I can't do anything.

HEATHER: He has to let you go to school. That's like, illegal if he doesn't. It's so illegal.

CHARLOTTE: I know. Is every dad like this? Is your dad like this?

HEATHER: No. Like he's weird and all? But he lets me drive? And I don't have a license or anything. And sometimes like I'm all: Can I borrow your credit card? And he's like: Why? And I'm all: So I can by some clothes? And he's like: Sure. And I totally use his credit card. I love him.

CHARLOTTE: That's like perfect.

HEATHER: He listens to Neil Diamond. That is not perfect.

CHARLOTTE: I like Neil Diamond.

HEATHER: No one likes Neil Diamond.

CHARLOTTE: I guess you're right.

HEATHER: I know I'm right.

CHARLOTTE: Heather? What would I do without you?

HEATHER: I don't know. Rot?

CHARLOTTE: Probably.

> (*Beat.*)

> I always wanted my name to be Caroline. Like Sweet Caroline.

HEATHER: There are so many better things to want.

CHARLOTTE: I guess.

HEATHER: Trust me. There are.

CHARLOTTE: Like what?

HEATHER: Like love. And fame. And a nice outfit. And a massage. And power. And power. And love. And love. And love. Also love.

CHARLOTTE: If I ever get out of here.

HEATHER: You'll get out.

CHARLOTTE: I will be so loved.

HEATHER: You will be.

CHARLOTTE: Everyone will want me.

HEATHER: I want you.

CHARLOTTE: Do you?

> (*Beat.*)

HEATHER: You know what you need? You need to like do something for you. Like go to a spa or something. You so deserve it. We should go. My dad'll pay.

CHARLOTTE: You're such a good friend.

HEATHER: I know.

CHARLOTTE: I love you Heather.

> (*Beat.*)

> We can do anything can't we? Like everyone says, 'You can do anything'. But that really means something with us, doesn't it?

HEATHER: It does.

CHARLOTTE: It so does.

> (*Beat.*)

HEATHER: Hey I'm really sorry about your mom.

CHARLOTTE: I know.

HEATHER: It's just so sad.

CHARLOTTE: I know.

HEATHER: Are you sad?

CHARLOTTE: Yeah.

HEATHER: Me too. She was so pretty. She was like, the best mom.

CHARLOTTE: I know.

HEATHER: With like the cupcakes? And the chicken pot pie? Oh my God, I loved your mother's chicken pot pie. It was like. Not even chicken. But. More than chicken. Or something. I don't know. It was just really good. I wish she was my mom.

CHARLOTTE: I know.

HEATHER: I wish my mom would die? 'Cause she's worthless? And that somehow, like in the next world or the afterlife or whatever, she would meet your mom, and like, send her back.

CHARLOTTE: Me too.

HEATHER: But it always happens to the beautiful ones Charlotte.

CHARLOTTE: What?

HEATHER: Early death.

CHARLOTTE: Really?

HEATHER: Of course. Everything beautiful dies. Only the ugly things stick around. That's why, if I live past thirty-five? I will be so upset.

CHARLOTTE: That is such a good point.

HEATHER: I know.

From

STEALING SWEETS AND PUNCHING PEOPLE

by Phil Porter

Stealing Sweets and Punching People *was first performed at the Latchmere Theatre, London, in October 2003.*

EMILY is sixteen years old, lives with her father and works in a junk shop, where MONICA is her boss. EMILY's mother died four years ago in a diving accident after EMILY told her it was a safe place to dive. Her guilt is so great that she regularly conjures up her mother's imaginary ghost and self-harms. Although her father still sees her as a little girl and treats her like one, EMILY is scared of losing him, particularly to MONICA who fancies him. MONICA is forty-six years old and runs her own junk/antiques/bric-a-brac shop. She hasn't had much luck with men and lives alone. In this scene, a new box of acquisitions has arrived in the shop and MONICA and EMILY are unpacking it.

EMILY/MONICA

(EMILY takes a mirror from the box and studies her face.)

EMILY: So much for the ugly duckling waking up as a beautiful swan.

MONICA: I don't know. A lot of girls would kill for bones like yours.

EMILY: Only a girl with no bones at all. My nose is identical to a white strawberry. My eyebrows are like a pair of hairy slugs on some kind of journey. If I had a face like the girl in the carpet shop –

MONICA: You'll be wishing for that skin back when you wake up flabby and dry and crumpled like me.

EMILY: I won't. I much prefer old faces. They remind me of things.

MONICA: Really? What does my face remind you of?

(EMILY studies MONICA's face.)

EMILY: It reminds me of…a half-collapsed house.

MONICA: Thank you so much.

EMILY: Or an underground cave or something. But I'd much rather that than have this greasy moon-face. It's not as if it pulls in crowds of boys.

MONICA: You can't expect boys to come flocking from nowhere and throw themselves at you.

EMILY: I wish they would.

MONICA: Sometimes you need to put yourself forward.

EMILY: But I do. I'm always thrusting myself forward. Okay, yesterday this nice-looking boy came in while you were out buying these. And he was flicking through the books and he had a silver flask, so I marched right up and asked him what was in it. But he just said soup. So I said 'Soup's not a meal,' because in my opinion it isn't, and he looked at me like I was covered in dog muck.

MONICA: Yeah. Maybe you put him on the spot a bit there.

EMILY: If he can't even cope with a girl like me –

MONICA: Or if you chose an easier topic like…television.

EMILY: There's a million things to say about soup.

MONICA: Or music. Or you could have asked him what he was looking for, or told him something interesting about something we sell. Or just asked a casual question like… 'Do you like the statue of the old man's head?'

EMILY: Do you like the statue of the old man's head?

MONICA: And told him it was carved by a one-handed sculptor.

EMILY: It was actually carved by a one-handed sculptor. He's not going to strip naked and jump on me because I go on about one-handed sculptors.

MONICA: No, but then you'd have a platform, wouldn't you. Once a conversation starts you have a platform to… I have no idea what I'm talking about.

EMILY: Monica!

MONICA: With my track record, you should be teaching me.

EMILY: Monica, you were just getting interesting.

(*They continue their work.*)

MONICA: All I was going to say… Once you have a platform conversation, then you have a chance to give off little signals. Don't you? You can use your body and operate in terms of body language. Reel in the fish.

EMILY: I don't know how to reel in the fish.

MONICA: Yes you do, follow your instincts.

EMILY: That's the problem. My instincts are as helpful as…nothing. The only thing that's natural to me is smiling like a wonky canoe. I need guidelines.

MONICA: You do not need guidelines from me.

EMILY: Yes I do.

MONICA: I am the last person.

(*They continue their work.*)

EMILY: Should I put my fingers up my nose? How do I reel in the fish, Monica?

MONICA: Just…little things.

EMILY: What little things?

MONICA: I don't know. Just the feminine things that women do to start to draw attention to their bodies.

EMILY: Which are?

MONICA: You might…play with your hair. Wind it into a spring around your finger. You know, like…

(*MONICA demonstrates the hair-winding technique. EMILY copies.*)

EMILY: I think he'd think I was a little bit demented.

(*EMILY experiments with the following techniques…*)

MONICA: Okay, you might stroke your neck or your wrists. Cross your legs at the top. And you might widen your eyes a bit. Look into his. Open your mouth a bit. Not quite as much as that. And you could tell him that he's interesting or looking good. Or lean across and touch him very slightly.

EMILY: With my hand?

MONICA: Just on the arm or the knee.

EMILY: (*Practising touching…*) What an interesting boy you are.

MONICA: And if you manage all of that and he's still not run away, then you're probably pretty much halfway there. Can you smell oranges?

(*Pause.*)

EMILY: Are those the tricks you try on my Dad, then?

MONICA: What do you mean?

EMILY: Or shouldn't I ask?

MONICA: I have never played tricks –

EMILY: Techniques then. Winding your hair in a spring and stroking your wrists. I'll keep my eyes peeled.

MONICA: Is that what you think?

EMILY: I'll tell him to watch out.

MONICA: I have never –

EMILY: Don't you dare, Monica. Don't you dare pretend you don't even like him because I heard the whole thing on the phone.

MONICA: You listen to me. I have absolutely no interest –

EMILY: You said you imagine he's your pillow! You said you had a dream where you were naked by a waterfall!

(*Pause.*)

MONICA: How dare you listen in.

EMILY: I wasn't.

MONICA: That is a private conversation.

EMILY: You were shouting your head off.

MONICA: I was not speaking about your dad.

EMILY: What other Mick then? The only other Mick you know is the butcher. If you fancy a bloke with bits of raw bacon in his beard, you deserve to be shot.

(*Pause.*)

MONICA: You're being very stupid and very confused.

EMILY: I'm not being stupid.

(*EMILY puts an item on the shelf.*)

I'd sooner die than have my dad shifted away from me.

From

FALLING
by Shelley Silas

The world premiere of Falling *took place at the Bush Theatre, London in November 2002.*

LINDA is forty-two years old and has been trying to get pregnant for the past seven years with her partner, Pete. They've just miscarried for the fifth time and she's thinking about giving up and getting on with the rest of her life, however painful that may be. GRACE is LINDA's niece who has come to stay. She's sixteen years old and announces that she's pregnant to a boy she doesn't love. She doesn't want to keep the baby and offers it to LINDA. However, LINDA doesn't want somebody else's baby, she wants her own. She also wants GRACE to think twice about an abortion because she may never have another chance to get pregnant. LINDA had an abortion when she was younger, thinking that there would be time to do it 'properly' at a later stage; however, time ran out. This scene takes place outside on LINDA and Pete's patio. GRACE is sitting on an upturned plant pot. She turns around and sees LINDA watching her.

GRACE/LINDA

GRACE: How long have you been watching me?

(*Beat.*)

LINDA: Since about two hours after you were born.

GRACE: That long?

LINDA: Yeah.

(*Beat.*)

GRACE: What was it like, seeing me as a baby?

LINDA: I burst into tears the first time I saw you.

GRACE: Because I was so ugly?

LINDA: Because I couldn't believe how small you were. And because you'd come out of my sister's body.

GRACE: Did she love me?

LINDA: Your mum? Yeah. Course.

GRACE: But she never wanted me?

LINDA: She didn't plan you, which isn't the same thing.

GRACE: But you make plans for things you want.

LINDA: And sometimes you get surprised. You get something else, something you thought you might not want or like or need. She got you. How fortunate is that. (*Beat.*) I heard this story, about new-born babies. Apparently, they know everything. They have total knowledge. And when they're born, this dip (*Pointing to the dip above her top lip.*) is filled out. The moment they're born, an angel puts his finger on that spot and a dip appears…and suddenly all their knowledge is gone…and they have to learn all over again.

GRACE: Is that true?

LINDA: If you want it to be.

(*Beat.*)

GRACE: I'm not ready to be a parent.

LINDA: I'm not ready to be anything. No one ever is.

GRACE: Really?

LINDA: We always planned to have a baby, not to not have one. We planned for the spare room to be the baby's room, not my office. Those walls were meant to be a different shade. There should have been a cot and a musical mobile and the smell should have been sweet, not musty from old books.

(*Beat.*)

GRACE: His name's Ryan. He's eighteen. He's a mechanic. He doesn't love me.

LINDA: Did he say?

GRACE: He said, I don't love you.

LINDA: Do you love him?

GRACE: Don't know. Don't think so. Isn't it meant to hurt down here (*Pointing to below her stomach.*) when you're in love?

LINDA: At first. Then it just becomes more of a dull ache. I thought you said he loved you? Before, you said someone said they loved you. Wasn't it him?

(*GRACE shakes her head.*)

GRACE: I can't imagine it.

LINDA: What?

GRACE: Having a baby. Giving birth to a shrivelled up piece of me and some bloke I don't even like, who smells of diesel and tobacco and thinks a Thatcherite is someone who fixes roofs.

(*Beat.*)

LINDA: You don't want it?

GRACE: I do. (*Beat.*) Just not now.

LINDA: Then when?

GRACE: When it's right.

LINDA: It might never be right.

GRACE: When I meet someone I love. Really love. Who loves me.

LINDA: What if you don't?

GRACE: I will. Everyone meets at least one person in a lifetime.

LINDA: That's it then?

GRACE: Yeah. That's it. I'm making an appointment.

LINDA: Where?

GRACE: At a Clinic.

LINDA: Grace.

GRACE: I don't want it. You don't want it.

LINDA: I didn't say that.

GRACE: Do you want it?

LINDA: No.

GRACE: See.

LINDA: It's different.

GRACE: It's a baby isn't it?

LINDA: It's your baby.

GRACE: What's wrong with my baby?

LINDA: It's yours.

GRACE: Then tell me to keep it. Tell me that getting rid of it is the wrong thing to do.

LINDA: I can't.

GRACE: Go on. Go on Linda. Tell me.

(*GRACE exits. LINDA's eyes glisten and fill with tears.*)

From

INSIDE OUT
by Tanika Gupta

Inside Out *was first performed at the Salisbury Playhouse in October 2002.*

AFFY and DI are sisters who looked out for each other in a violent family home. Their mother, Chloe, was a prostitute with a violent pimp/boyfriend who beat the girls and sexually abused DI. Both girls have different fathers: DI is mixed race and AFFY is white. After a particularly bad beating, AFFY contacted her real father and he moved her away to live with him in Brighton. DI was left with her mother and, during a struggle, she stabbed and killed her. When DI is released from prison five years later, she travels to Brighton to see AFFY with whom she has lost contact (AFFY refused to visit her after their mother was killed). DI is now twenty-two years old and AFFY is twenty. Much to her surprise, DI learns that AFFY now has two children.

AFFY/DI

AFFY: Must have been lonely in prison.

DI: I made friends.

AFFY: Where 'you staying?

DI: Mate's house in Manchester. Kipping on her floor.

AFFY: You came all the way down from Manchester?

DI: Don't worry – I'm not gonna crash here. I got another mate, lives nearby. Said I could stay at hers.

Start work next week.

AFFY: You've only been out a week and you've already got a job?

DI: It's only bar work – my mate fixed it up for me. Her brother runs a bar.

AFFY: You seem to have a lot of friends.

DI: Lots of friends in low places. Bar work isn't exactly the way I want to go but it's a start.

(*AFFY pulls out a carton of cigarettes. She offers one to DI.*)

Thanks, but I don't smoke.

(*AFFY lights up.*)

I hear they knocked our old house down?

AFFY: Built new flats.

DI: Would've liked to have seen the place again.

(*A baby cries from the back room. DI looks startled. AFFY gets up.*)

AFFY: I'll just settle her.

(*AFFY bustles out of the room. DI looks amazed. She notices a toy tucked under the settee. She picks it up and turns it in her hand. AFFY returns.*)

I think she was having a bad dream.

DI: You've got a baby?

AFFY: Yeah.

DI: I never knew.

AFFY: Actually, I've got two.

DI: Can I see them?

AFFY: I'd rather you didn't – they'd get scared if they saw a stranger in their bedroom.

DI: How old are they?

AFFY: The little one's six months – that's Katie – and Kiren's two.

DI: You have been busy.

(*AFFY takes some photos out and shows them to DI.*)

Fuck Affy – you're a mum. That's amazing.

(*AFFY smiles for the first time.*)

AFFY: Not getting much sleep but they're both gorgeous. Kiren's just starting to talk. Says 'Mummy', 'Daddy' and Thomas.

DI: Thomas?

AFFY: Thomas the Tank Engine.

(*DI laughs.*)

And Katie's sitting up on her own, with lots of cushions stuffed behind her. Sometimes she keels over and falls flat on her face.

DI: She looks just like you did when you were a baby.

AFFY: You think?

DI: Oh yeah – especially round the eyes.

AFFY: She's got her dad's sticky out ears.

DI: I didn't like to say.

(*They laugh.*)

AFFY: They're lovely kids.

DI: Do they even know they've got an auntie?

AFFY: No.

DI: And Sean? He know about my existence?

(*Beat.*

AFFY doesn't answer, but looks away.

DI looks upset for the first time.)

Must be tough looking after two kids.

AFFY: Yeah. Most of the time it is me on my own. Sean's always working. He's a hospital porter during the day.

(*AFFY lapses into silence.*)

DI: So, didn't you get through your exams?

AFFY: Too many other things to worry about. Once the kids are up and running – maybe I'll go back to college. I feel like I owe it to Dad. How did you cope inside?

DI: I got through it.

AFFY: Is it as nasty as they say it is?

DI: Yes and no. It's the boredom and the petty regulations that get to you more than anything else.

AFFY: Must be a bit scary being out.

DI: It's more exciting. Feel like I'm holding my breath all the time trying to stop myself.

AFFY: Stop yourself?

DI: From going over the top. Laughing like a maniac, crying like an idiot – that sort of thing. Got to hold it in.

From

MERCY FINE
by Shelley Silas

Mercy Fine *was first performed by Clean Break Theatre Company in 2005. The tour included: Birmingham Repertory Theatre, York Theatre Royal, Salisbury Playhouse, Southwark Playhouse and various women's prisons.*

After MERCY's Indian father left, her mother took up with a new man who treated the two of them appallingly. MERCY's mother ended up killing him but MERCY pleaded guilty to protect her and was imprisoned. When the play opens, she has served nine years of her sentence and is due for release in the next 24 hours. She confesses to her friend, Viv, that she is scared about going back to the real world and coping on her own. Whilst in prison, MERCY has been released once a week, with another prisoner, FREHIA, to work in the local charity shop. On her last day MERCY was spat upon by somebody in the street and called 'a fucking coon'. She spat back and is now terrified that the Governor will not release her because of the incident. MERCY runs on in a panic followed by FREHIA. They stop at the entrance to the Governor's office.

MERCY/FREHIA

MERCY: Fuck, fuck, fuck. Just go will you.

FREHIA: I want to help.

MERCY: You can't help. Just go.

FREHIA: What you gonna do, Mercy?

MERCY: Tell him what happened.

FREHIA: Yeah. That's good. Tell him what happened. Tell him it was an accident. You were provoked. Yeah, provoked.

MERCY: Piss off will you Frehia.

FREHIA: That's nice. I only want to help. I was there. I saw it.

MERCY: Yeah, you and everyone else. Glaring at me like I'm some specimen.

FREHIA: It's no big deal. It ain't a crime.

MERCY: Anything I do is a crime. You don't get it do you?

FREHIA: I got words Mercy Fine. They may not always be the right words, but I got them. And I got eyes.

MERCY: And who do you think they're going to believe? The eyes and ears of a good girl, or the eyes and ears of a bad one?

FREHIA: I ain't bad. I like the juice too much, that's all. And sometimes I mix my juice. And sometimes I get behind the wheel of someone else's car and let the juice take over.

MERCY: One day you'll kill someone.

FREHIA: Like you did?

(*Pause.*)

Let me come with you.

MERCY: You just don't know when to stop.

FREHIA: It slipped out.

MERCY: Viv's the only one who keeps her mouth shut. All the time I've been in here, she's never once asked me why I'm here.

FREHIA: But she knows.

MERCY: She's never asked me.

FREHIA: Is that why you're friends? Is that why you tell her everything?

MERCY: Not everything.

FREHIA: I keep my mouth shut.

MERCY: You? No one ever knows what's going to come out of your mouth.

FREHIA: They call me spontaneous. (*Beat.*) Come on. Let's practice what you're gonna say. Like role-playing.

MERCY: I'm not an actor.

FREHIA: Yeah you are. We all are. You, me, Viv's the biggest actor of the lot.

(*MERCY shakes her head like she can't believe what she's about to do. FREHIA coughs. When she speaks her voice is lower than usual.*)

Mercy Fine. What have you done?

MERCY: I'm not doing it if you put on an idiot's voice.

(*FREHIA does her usual voice.*)

FREHIA: It's Governor Smith.

MERCY: That is not Governor Smith. And if he hears you doing that you'll get your privileges taken away. Hurry up.

FREHIA: What happened?

MERCY: It was an accident.

FREHIA: An accident?

MERCY: Yeah.

FREHIA: Governor Smith…

MERCY: Governor Smith.

FREHIA: Tell me what occurred?

MERCY: Occurred? What kind of word is that?

FREHIA: That's what he'd say. Occurred. He likes to feel clever.

MERCY: Well, sir, what occurred, was this. We were walking to the shop.

FREHIA: Which shop?

MERCY: You know which shop.

FREHIA: I do. But Governor Smith doesn't.

MERCY: The charity shop.

FREHIA: Which charity?

MERCY: Frehia!

FREHIA: Governor Smith is into details.

MERCY: Geranium shop. For the blind.

FREHIA: I see. (*Beat.*) What were you doing?

MERCY: I'd just parked the car. (*Beat.*) I'd just parked the car, and we were walking to the shop.

FREHIA: Was that girl there?

MERCY: Which girl?

FREHIA: The pretty one.

> (*MERCY can't think who the pretty girl is.*)

> Frehia Andrews.

MERCY: Yes, she was there.

FREHIA: She's one of the good ones you know.

MERCY: Really.

FREHIA: Yeah. Since she converted, well, she's changed.

MERCY: But she still drinks. And drives. What do you think of that Governor Smith?

FREHIA: Hey, I'll ask the questions.

MERCY: Frehia, this is about me, not you. If you want to help me, fine, if not, go and annoy someone else.

FREHIA: Tell me what happened.

MERCY: We were walking to the shop. This woman comes up to me, from nowhere, and she looks at me. Stares at me.

> (*Beat.*)

FREHIA: Then what?

MERCY: She calls me a fucking coon.

FREHIA: And?

MERCY: She spits in my face.

FREHIA: What did you do?

MERCY: I spat back. I couldn't help it.

FREHIA: What you did was wrong.

MERCY: I know.

FREHIA: And if someone from the shop hadn't told us, were you going to?

MERCY: Of course. (*Beat.*) The thing is, if I didn't do that, I might have…punched her.

FREHIA: Don't say that.

MERCY: And I was never violent before coming here.

FREHIA: You killed someone before coming here. (*Beat.*) It wasn't me saying that, it was Governor Smith. (*Beat.*) Haven't we taught you anything Mercy Fine?

MERCY: You've taught me how to be angry and pissed off and hateful. You put us lot together and sometimes, you bring out the worst in us. You're meant to prepare us for the world, but you prepare us for shit. You know that? You prepare us for shit. You send us to anger management and you know what, I come out feeling more angry than when I went in. And I am not an angry person.

FREHIA: Don't say that.

From

CATCH

by April de Angelis, Stella Feehily, Tanika Gupta, Chloe Moss and Laura Wade

Catch *was commissioned by The Royal Court Theatre in London and opened there in December 2006.*

Catch explores the notions of 'identity' and 'surveillance' in contemporary society, where we are categorised on national databases by even our smallest actions (how often do you buy a toothbrush?). CLAIRE is an 'identity actualiser' at the head of a company called Chrysalis Identity Solutions. She is described as 'thirty-five and black' and helps people improve their social standing by changing how they live and shop. However, CLAIRE has some identity issues of her own, exacerbated by some traumatic experiences, and soon her own life will begin to unravel. CAROL is a single mother in her late twenties and one of CLAIRE's private clients who needs to improve her place in society in order to access credit. They are meeting in CLAIRE's office.

CLAIRE/CAROL

CLAIRE: Carol.

CAROL: This is a bit you know a bit

CLAIRE: Terribly sorry. I over-ran.

CAROL: I only put seven quid in the meter,

That's exactly an hour and a quarter, and it's a fifteen minute walk from here.

The baby's nappy is rank and I don't have a change.

She'll be screaming the place down in a minute.

CLAIRE: I'll be as brief as possible.

CAROL: Brief is not what I'm expecting.

(*CLAIRE takes out documents from CAROL's file.*)

CLAIRE: One moment.

(*CAROL picks up an invitation that is on CLAIRE's desk.*)

CAROL: Covent Garden.

You going?

CLAIRE: Emm yes. I hope to.

CAROL: César Franck.

He was underrated in his time.

CLAIRE: You like classical?

CAROL: Surprised?

CLAIRE: Not at all.

CAROL: You are.

I used to work for the head of classical at Sony.

Five years I cleaned for him.

Gave me little invites here and there.

Filthy bastard though. Smoked in the bath and stubbed his butts out in the soap dish.

CLAIRE: Did you bring the documentation?

(*CAROL digs in her bag and pulls out a pile of crumpled papers.*)

CAROL: (*Handing her another letter.*) And here's a doctor's letter.

About my depression.

It's not easy you know. I'm a single mum.

CLAIRE: I understand.

CAROL: So. What's the deal?

CLAIRE: Right. I've worked out a feasible start-up strategy.

There was one problem.

The video footage, CCTV?

CAROL: Told you –

I was a minor.

Got let off easy. The court took into consideration that my foster parents were evil bastards.

CLAIRE: I didn't locate that information. Your record is all that exists.

And though we can sculpt your future, we can't erase your past.

CAROL: Have you seen the tapes?

CLAIRE: No. But they're out there.

CAROL: I know my rights.

If stuff is out there I should be able to see it. For God's sake it's just a bit of shoplifting.

CLAIRE: You're absolutely right.

Shall we go through your file? It's rather a tome.

CAROL: A what?

CLAIRE: A fifty-page file. Information existing in the database on you.

CAROL: Fifty pages on me?

(*CLAIRE clicks on a link on her computer.*

She scrolls down as she reads from the screen.)

CLAIRE: Uses Colgate toothpaste. Change of toothbrush approx every twenty-four months. Doesn't floss. Future dental issues. Food: fish fingers, oven chips, chicken nuggets, Cornflakes. Possible future health issues.

Smokes Benson and Hedges.

CAROL: I'm trying to give up.

CLAIRE: Suspected stomach ulcer.

Self-medicates with Gaviscon.

Drinks lager. A likely binge drinker.

Promiscuous.

CAROL: You what?

CLAIRE: There's a glitch in the system.

If you've purchased any over-the-counter cystitis or thrush treatments, you instantly fall into that group.

CAROL: Fuck's sake.

CLAIRE: It not only cites the anti-anxiety pills you've been on since 1999 but video shop fines, a failed payment on mail order catalogue purchases and an altercation with a woman from British Gas.

CAROL: That trout. Trying to charge me the previous tenant's bill.

But I won that war.

CLAIRE: You did – however these records (among others) class you in category E-F.

CAROL: I knew it.

CLAIRE: That's why you've had difficulty with getting credit, Mortgages, chequebook. That's why you've been discriminated against in the workplace.

CAROL: But none of it adds up to who I am.

CLAIRE: It's never about 'who you are' – but 'who you appear to be'.

We need to get you moved up to super classification C. Grade C2.

CAROL: So what do I do?

CLAIRE: Simple changes to your consumer profile.

Shopping preferences?

Iceland is definitely out. I'll come back to that in a bit. More importantly; address. You must think about changing from council to rented.

CAROL: Are you for real?

CLAIRE: Two blocks from your road? Same area, different postcode, but different profile.

Your profile shifts? Your circumstances shift. You with me?

CAROL: Yeah. Yeah I am.

CLAIRE: (*Handing her a folder.*) Enclosed is a list of properties within your price range and area. A Chrysalis employee will accompany you to any viewings –

CAROL: It's such a lot to take in.

CLAIRE: Carol, I truly believe in personal power.

I believe we can change our circumstances, become masters of our own destinies, no matter what hand life has dealt us.

It's about choice. And sometimes we need a little help to make the right choices.

The aim of the sessions is to guide you to actualise your potential, to encourage your social grading upwards.

So we start by managing your profile.

CAROL: In 'The Great – Out There'.

CLAIRE: Exactly and it may feel a bit overwhelming – but rest assured – we will go at your pace. As I said in our first meeting – you talk and I will listen.

(*The baby starts to cry.*)

CAROL: I'm not sure I can afford to go 'at my pace'.

Shut up Robin will ya.

(*CLAIRE moves round to have a look at the baby.*

CAROL rummages about the baby.)

Oh bloody brilliant. No dummy either.

From

GET UP AND TIE YOUR FINGERS
by Ann Coburn

Get Up and Tie Your Fingers *was first performed in Eyemouth in October 1995 and throughout the Scottish Borders by Fourth Wall Productions as part of the Borders Festival.*

On 14th October 1881 forty-five fishing boats set out from Eyemouth harbour, heart of the Scottish Borders' fishing industry. The freak storm that followed took the lives of one hundred and twenty-nine men; fathers, brothers and sons, all from the one community. *Get Up and Tie Your Fingers* tells the story from the women's viewpoint. JEAN is in her late thirties/early forties and is married to one of the fishermen. She has two children, Billie and MOLLY, who is fifteen years old. MOLLY yearns to get away from the village but her mother has other ideas. This scene takes place before the storm and JEAN is trying to prepare MOLLY for her work as part of a fish-gutting crew. She must learn to tie her fingers to protect them from the gutting knife.

JEAN/MOLLY

JEAN: Right, let's see you tie your fingers.

> (*MOLLY approaches the table, every inch of her showing her reluctance, and begins to wrap her fingers in the bandage strips.*)

No, no, no! Far too slow. You've to wrap them quick and tie them tight.

MOLLY: Oh, I cannae do it! Why do I have to practise, mam? Why cannae you or Janet tie them for me?

JEAN: We willnae have the time once the season is upon us. When the fleet comes in at dawn with enough herring to fill up the harbour, me and Janet'll be too busy getting ourselves ready.

MOLLY: – Oh, to fill up the harbour…

JEAN: Aye, and Mr Sinclair'll send the caller to rouse us from our beds –

> (*MOLLY interrupts, imitating the sing-song voice of the caller.*)

MOLLY: Get up and tie your fingers!

JEAN: – for he'll want it gutted, salted, sorted and into barrels while it's still fresh enough to wink an eye at you. Now, Molly, as soon as you hear the caller, you've to get down to the curing yards, otherwise me and Janet'll be gutting without a packer, do you see?

MOLLY: But enough herring to fill the harbour! Think how many that is.

JEAN: Molly! Forget the fish. I'm trying to tell you you're part of a crew now. You need to be speedy! Can you do that?

MOLLY: Yes, mam.

JEAN: Let's see you, then.

> (*MOLLY picks up the first bandage strip again and wraps it around her finger. JEAN stands, arms folded, watching her and soon MOLLY starts to fumble. She finishes wrapping the first finger and attempts to tie a knot.*)

No, no, no! What did I tell you? Use your teeth. To tie the knot!

> (*MOLLY does so, clumsily, and becoming increasingly distressed by her mother's critical attention.*)

Oh, see? See? Why, your Da was a fool to let you stay on at school! Three pennies a week we've had to pay. Three pennies! And for what?

(*MOLLY silently mouths 'Three pennies a week' in unison with JEAN while her back is turned.*)

MOLLY: – Spinning globes – shiny maps – the Empire painted red –

JEAN: – I told him it was a waste of money and good working years. It's too late to teach a great lump of a girl like you. You're nearly a woman, so you are! Ach, your Da is as soft as river mud over you.

MOLLY: (*Ripping off the bandage strips.*) My Da is not soft!

JEAN: You two. All right. (*She places three baskets and a pile of kindling on or beside the table.*) Prove it. Show me all that extra schooling has not ruined you for work.

MOLLY: Yes, mam.

JEAN: Now, you've seen the lassies working down in the yards. Did you mind how they sorted the herring into sizes as they gutted, ready for the barrels?

MOLLY: Yes, mam.

JEAN: (*She points to the baskets.*) These are the herring barrels, and… (*She points to the kindling.*) …these are herring.

(*MOLLY giggles. JEAN rounds on her.*)

Oh, what is it now, you flighty wee thing?

MOLLY: Mam. Those herring'll not pass the fisheries inspector.

JEAN: Molly!

MOLLY: Where are they bound, mam? Where will the barrels go?

JEAN: Russia. Now –

MOLLY: Russia! They have palaces and churches there with roofs made of gold and shaped like turnips. Think of that, mam! All those golden 'neeps shining in the sun. Oh, I'd like to see that –

JEAN: Molly! Size them. Call them as you sort.

(*Sighing, MOLLY selects pieces of kindling and throws them into one of the three baskets, according to their size.*)

MOLLY: That's a Mattie, that's a Full, that's a half-full, that's another Mattie – Ow! And that's a splinter.

JEAN: Now, see. That's why you need to tie your fingers… If that'd been your gutting knife, you'd be cut to the bone now and no use to anyone. A deep wound with the salt in it won't mend in a hurry… (*She bends over MOLLY's hand and removes the splinter but then, in a rare moment of tenderness, she does not let go. Instead she strokes her daughter's fingers.*) Soft hands, see. They'll toughen up, right enough.

MOLLY: (*Turning their hands over to look at JEAN's palms.*) Oh, mam. Look at the scars on your poor hands, all purple and swollen…

JEAN: Don't feel sorry for me, lass. Proud of these hands I am. They show how hard I work.

(*MOLLY is made brave by her mother's rare gentleness.*)

MOLLY: Mam? I – I – When I dwell on what it means to be a fishwife, with a man and his bairns all looking to me for food and care, and the work… Oh, mam, I get such a tightening here – (*She presses their clasped hands to her breastbone.*) – as though the air has clotted up inside me. It hurts, mam. It feels like drowning…

JEAN: Whisht, child. You mustnae fret so. Every fisher lassie doubts herself when she sees the work ahead. But they all learn to manage, for they come from good, strong stock. Aye, they are bred to it. Besides, no young fishwife is ever alone – do y'ken? And, Molly lass, don't pay any mind to my blethering. You could do the work, if you would only put your heart into it.

MOLLY: No, mam, no! I cannae put my heart into it, for I don't want it. I don't want the gutting and the bait gathering and never the time to lift my head and look about me. When I think of marrying Angus and living out my whole life here, I – (*She bangs her clasped hands against her breastbone in an attempt to demonstrate her feelings of suffocation.*) Mam… I want to see further than our harbour wall.

JEAN: Well! Then you are a silly, wicked girl!

MOLLY: Mam –

JEAN: We are needed here, Molly. No man could be a fisher without a wife! Remember that. And don't you be so quick to turn your nose up at Janet's boy. You are lucky any lad wants to wed you, the way you drift aboot.

MOLLY: Mam, I like Angus fine! But… I don't know if I love him –

JEAN: Love? You want love, too? Now, you listen to me, Mollie. This is the life you were born to. You cannae throw it off like an old shawl. What else could you turn to?

MOLLY: (*Frightened by her mother's anger, but still trying to make her point.*) Mam, I – I thought, if the minister would write me a letter, I could go to work for a Lady. They have grand houses in Edinburgh, mam, and in London – even over the sea…a – and sometimes, when they travel, they take their best maids with them –

JEAN: Hah! So, you think if you curtsey prettily enough, you'll catch your Lady's eye and she'll up and take you jaunting alongside her?

MOLLY: Aye, I do. Oh, mam, I'd look after her so well she'd have to take me, for she'd not manage without me.

JEAN: You wee fool! Your Lady'd never set eyes on you for you'd never leave the kitchen. You'd be set on as a scullery maid, just like poor, wee Annie Dougal. I'll give you seeing further! How far is Annie seeing now, in her little wooden box in the kirkyard?

MOLLY: But, mam –

JEAN: Mollie, no lass of mine is going into service and there's an end to it!

MOLLY: Then I shall do nothing. My Da will keep me out of the yards if I ask him to. I know he will.

JEAN: Your Da will do no such thing!

MOLLY: *My* Da willnae make me do something I hate. He loves me. (*She pauses, then repeats the phrase more deliberately.*) He loves *me.*

(*Infuriated, JEAN slaps MOLLY across the face. MOLLY claps her hand to her cheek. They stand glaring at one another, breathing hard then MOLLY turns her back.*)

From

CONCEALMENT
by Reza de Wet

Concealment *was first performed in May 2004 in the Box
Theatre at the Rhodes University Theatre complex. It was
produced by Rhodes Drama Department on the occasion of the
university's Centenary celebrations.*

Concealment is set in one of England's colonial outposts in South
Africa during the 19th Century. AMY and her father travel out
from England to retrieve AMY's sister, MAY, who was recently
widowed. MAY's husband was an English missionary working
in the region and received a fatal head wound after collapsing
from exposure whilst out walking in the hottest part of the day
without his hat. AMY and her father are disturbed to find MAY
untouched by grief, unwilling to return and drawn instead to
the wild, natural beauty of her moonlit garden. This scene is
set in a part of the garden with a garden bench and AMY enters
from the house.

AMY/MAY

AMY: It's very late. Won't you come to bed?

MAY: Not yet.

(*Short silence.*)

AMY: Do you mind…if I sit?

(*Short silence. AMY sits.*)

Lovely cool air after the heat.

(*Short silence.*)

I really don't know how you've managed it.

MAY: What do you mean?

AMY: Such a lovely garden in this dry, desolate place.

MAY: Yes. But there is a borehole you see. Endless water bubbling out of it.

AMY: How fortunate.

MAY: And then it's mostly Samuel of course.

AMY: Samuel?

MAY: Yes. He knows so much. He plants everything at night.

AMY: How extraordinary.

MAY: When the moon is waxing or when it's full.

AMY: And he believes…that it makes a difference does he?

MAY: Yes he does. Oh, my hem is all wet and muddy.

(*AMY gives a little laugh. AMY continues to look at MAY who is moving about the garden distractedly.*)

AMY: I see…that you're not wearing mourning. Oh…I realise that in a place like this it might be difficult…

(*Short silence.*)

But…you might at least wear something a little…more muted in tone.

MAY: It offends you does it?

AMY: It's just…that it's hardly suitable.

MAY: Well at least you are dressed very suitably and soberly. And I suppose that is how it should be.

AMY: What do you mean?

MAY: I know you've always been so fond of him. After all it was you who introduced us.

AMY: I hardly remember.

MAY: (*Sitting down next to her.*) But surely. I mean…it was quite an occasion. He was the first man you ever brought home to tea.

AMY: A friend. He was only a friend.

MAY: But of course. I'm merely saying that you were very fond of him. After all you have so much in common. Your many charitable deeds. (*Little laugh.*) Your interest…in the essayists… (*Short silence.*)

AMY: All those evenings when John visited us…you never said anything.

MAY: What should I have said?

AMY: That you were in love with him, surely.

MAY: Well…I was hardly that. I was fond of him of course. We all were.

AMY: But…if you married him?

MAY: I told him quite plainly. He said I would come to care for him in time. And then of course he was so desperately set on me.

AMY: But why John? If you didn't have any…particular feelings for him? You could have had anyone.

MAY: (*Little laugh.*) And where would I have found him? You know…how jealously father guarded my virtue. No man was good enough. (*Little laugh.*) But he didn't mind John.

(*AMY turns her head away.*)

Oh, but…after a while, I did care for him. A good deal. And I began to respect and admire him. Very deeply.

(*Short silence.*)

AMY: He was such a good man. So much he could still have done.

MAY: Quite right. (*Short silence.*) If only he hadn't lost his hat. Well, he might still have been alive. You know, it was the most hideously hot day we'd had all year. Even early in the morning one could hardly breathe. Even the slight breeze felt like fumes from a furnace. I closed the shutters and stayed in bed. But he…walked a long way…without a hat…in the midday sun. I don't know why he had to do that.

AMY: Surely you're not blaming him? I'm quite sure it was a call of duty. His own welfare would have been his least concern. I know him. (*Little intake of breath.*) Knew him.

MAY: It was hardly a matter of urgency. He might have waited a few hours at least. He was only going to have a conversation with a missionary. (*Softly.*) At midday.

AMY: (*Distressed.*) But what are you trying to say?

MAY: Nothing, nothing at all. It's just all…so unnecessary.

AMY: (*Rather stiffly.*) Poor May. It must have been such a shock.

MAY: Yes. I waited and waited that evening. Until very late. I was becoming quite frantic. At last…I sent Samuel to look for him.

AMY: Don't think about it any more. It will only distress you.

MAY: I told you that when he hit his head when he collapsed from the heat. He had… (*Falters. Touches her forehead.*) the most terrible wound.

AMY: (*Rising.*) I'll go in now. I really need some sleep.

From

MAD MARGARET'S REVENGE
by Lesley Ross

Mad Margaret's Revenge *was first performed at the Hong Kong fringe club as part of The International Festival of Lilliput in November 2002. It is published in a volume of short plays by Lesley Ross entitled* The Jolly Folly of Polly, the Scottish Trolley Dolly and Other Mini-Marvels.

MARGARET is a woman with a large frame who has worked for some time at the local grocery store. She was hoping for the manager's job there but Peter Mervins (whom she once slept with) was promoted above her. She feels her life is a big disappointment and secretly thinks about directing movies as an escape. GEMMA is one of her imaginary creations (younger, slimmer and prettier) with whom she can talk to about her ideas and disappointments. Together they construct numerous film versions of MARGARET's life.

GEMMA/MARGARET

GEMMA: Why don't you become a film director?

MARGARET: What?

GEMMA: You've got real talent, you tell great stories, why don't you write one?

MARGARET: Wouldn't know where to begin, would I? I'm good at peas: I know where the peas go.

GEMMA: Yeah.

MARGARET: You're looking for peas, Madam, aisle four.

GEMMA: Aisle four.

MARGARET: By the cauliflower cheese. Lovely.

GEMMA: What about him?

MARGARET: What, Peter Mervins? (*Thinks.*) Screw him, and his promotion. My promotion. I quit. I've had enough (*Beat.*) What?

GEMMA: I didn't mean Peter. I meant *him*.

MARGARET: Oh, yeah I could easily write a movie about *him*. He was lovely.

GEMMA: Lovely.

MARGARET: Lovely.

GEMMA: (*Beat.*) Where would you set it?

MARGARET: Where would I set it?

GEMMA: Yeah?

MARGARET: Well… At the fairground.

GEMMA: Okay, yeah, that's obvious. But when?

MARGARET: Er… New Year's Eve.

GEMMA: Liking it.

MARGARET: Um… And he's Spanish.

GEMMA: Nice. Makes him seem more desirable and mysterious.

MARGARET: And our heroine, Gemma.

GEMMA: Jodie?

MARGARET: Gemma, she's up in Birmingham with her childhood friend Mary and she falls in love with this bloke on this ride called the Chinese Dragon.

GEMMA: This huge metallic monstrosity that spins you in a million different ways.

MARGARET: Spins you till you're sick!

GEMMA: And he works on this ride?

MARGARET: Yes, and he's called Antonio, and he just keeps noticing her.

GEMMA: Long shot of her getting off the car at the end of the ride.

MARGARET: And he's still smiling at her.

GEMMA: Close up of this gorgeous Spaniard.

MARGARET: Gorgeous.

GEMMA: He's even got a part in the new Bond movie.

MARGARET: What?

GEMMA: I was elaborating, sorry.

MARGARET: No, no, it's good when you elaborate.

GEMMA: Really?

MARGARET: Yes, especially when you don't. Okay?

GEMMA: Sorry. Keep going.

MARGARET: Antonio knows that she's the one for him. It's there, it's…well, chemistry. She's his angel. He jumps from the ride.

GEMMA: The camera following him as he goes.

MARGARET: For nearly a minute of film, the Beatles playing on the soundtrack, he searches for her, searching for the woman that may change his life, through the New Year's Eve revellers, searching. Suddenly we hear people chanting.

BOTH: 5, 4, 3, 2, 1 – Happy new year!

MARGARET: Long shot of fireworks, a champagne cork blows, and then he sees her, soft focus, as her hair is lit by the neon lights of the ride behind her.

GEMMA: Gemma's friend Mary is kissing someone she's never met before.

MARGARET: One of the extras.

GEMMA: And then Gemma turns her face and stares at him.

MARGARET: The camera shoots between them as they move in towards each other, people singing 'Auld Lang Syne' in the background. The angels kiss. He says 'Swindon, 4th January'. She looks at him meekly.

GEMMA: Soft focus, once more.

MARGARET: 'I'll be there.'

　(*Beat.*)

GEMMA: Says Gemma.

MARGARET: (*Beat.*) What? Oh, yes, says Gemma.

GEMMA: I'll be there.

MARGARET: So, do you like it?

GEMMA: I love it. Write it, go on write it!

MARGARET: Where've I got time to write a bloody movie? I've hardly got time to separate the full fat from the semi-skimmed.

From

THE BOGUS WOMAN
by Kay Adshead

Commissioned by the Red Room, The Bogus Woman *was first
performed as a work in progress at Waterman's Arts Centre
in June 2000. The play premiered at the Traverse Theatre,
Edinburgh, in August 2000 and was subsequently performed at
The Bush Theatre, London, in February 2001.*

The Bogus Woman tells the story of a young African journalist
who was raped and her family murdered because of her writing.
She flees to England with false documents and is detained
at Campsfield and Tinsley House asylum centres, suffering
indignities and torment at the hands of government officials
and guards. Here, an INTERROGATOR questions her account of
what happened in an attempt to discover whether the YOUNG
WOMAN should be granted asylum in the United Kingdom. The
play was originally written to be performed by one actor but
can be adapted to include other performers.

INTERROGATOR/YOUNG WOMAN

INTERROGATOR:
And then they shot
your father is it?

YOUNG WOMAN:
No!
no!
my husband.

INTERROGATOR:
With a single shot?

YOUNG WOMAN:
No
they were spraying
bullets everywhere
by then

INTERROGATOR:
Really?
And yet you yourself
escaped
all those bullets?

YOUNG WOMAN:
(*Halting.*) I was lower down
on a day bed,
I don't think
they'd seen me then

and…
my husband…

INTERROGATOR:
Acted as a shield,
yes thank you.
Now they killed
your father with a bayonet

am I right?

YOUNG WOMAN:
Yes

INTERROGATOR:
How extraordinary.
Why take the trouble
of suddenly bayoneting
someone
when you're in the middle
of spraying bullets
from your rifle.

YOUNG WOMAN:
They'd stopped shooting

INTERROGATOR:
Really?

YOUNG WOMAN:
Yes

INTERROGATOR:
And had the men
seen you yet?

YOUNG WOMAN:
I…

INTERROGATOR:
Yes?

YOUNG WOMAN:
I don't know

INTERROGATOR:
Well, was it
a very large room
you were in?

YOUNG WOMAN:
Not very large

INTERROGATOR:
It was morning,
presumably there was light?

YOUNG WOMAN:
Yes

INTERROGATOR:
So
why hadn't
they seen
you?

YOUNG WOMAN:
I…

INTERROGATOR:
Yes…?

YOUNG WOMAN:
I was partially hidden
behind a curtain.

INTERROGATOR:
A curtain?
Why didn't you mention
this before?

YOUNG WOMAN:
I…
I forgot
I didn't think
it was important.

INTERROGATOR:
So they suddenly
decided to stop shooting,
and bayonet
your father.

YOUNG WOMAN:
He'd screamed
don't you see
and sprang
at them

he surprised them.

INTERROGATOR:
An unarmed elderly man
'surprised'
three strapping youths

YOUNG WOMAN:
He shocked them
so they stopped shooting.

INTERROGATOR:
Where did they
bayonet your father,
on what part of the body?

YOUNG WOMAN:
Every part

INTERROGATOR:
And then
they calmly decided
to put the bayonets away
and shoot your mother?

YOUNG WOMAN:
(*Faltering, in difficulty.*) I…
Yes…

INTERROGATOR:
Then stop shooting again
and bayonet
your baby daughter.

YOUNG WOMAN:
(*Appears to have difficulty breathing.*) I…
I…

INTERROGATOR:
Perhaps
you'd like
to take
a sip
of water?

YOUNG WOMAN:
(*Very softly.*) my baby
wasn't killed
with bayonets,

the taller one

couldn't
get the bayonet
out of my
father's neck,

he killed
my baby
with his machete.

INTERROGATOR:
Now I'm confused

because it says in your notes
you gave birth to a baby
a few weeks later

    (*Pause.*)

YOUNG WOMAN:
(*Very tense, tearful, distraught.*) I was raped
by the soldiers
I…
miscarried a foetus
in a bucket
while hiding

INTERROGATOR:
Ah yes.
Are you quite sure of this?

YOUNG WOMAN:
(*Hesitant.*) Yes

INTERROGATOR:
I'm no doctor,
and we probably
need expert advice

but isn't it
highly unlikely
that you conceived
the day after
giving birth.

Is it possible?

YOUNG WOMAN:
I…

INTERROGATOR:
Or is it in fact a medical impossibility!

YOUNG WOMAN:
I…

INTERROGATOR:
You still insist you saw this
grinning foetus
in a bucket?

YOUNG WOMAN:
I…
yes…no…

INTERROGATOR:
Well did you or didn't you?

YOUNG WOMAN:
I…perhaps…I

INTERROGATOR:
I would suggest
you are lying

YOUNG WOMAN:
I…

INTERROGATOR:
I would suggest
you are lying

YOUNG WOMAN:
I…

INTERROGATOR:
I would suggest
your whole story,
the killing of your family
the rape
is nothing
but a pack
of well-schemed lies.

YOUNG WOMAN:
(*Almost shouting.*) I am not lying

From

CALCUTTA KOSHER
by Shelley Silas

Calcutta Kosher *was first performed at Theatre Royal Stratford East in June 2004 in association with Kali Theatre Company.*

Set in the dwindling Jewish community in Calcutta, this play tells the story of two sisters (ESTHER and SILVIE) who return to their crumbling childhood home to visit their mother. She not only reveals that she is dying but also that Maki, who grew up in the family home, is their half-sister. Maki was born out of a long term affair with a Hindu man, whom their now dead father never knew about. The news forces ESTHER and SILVIE to re-evaluate their own lives as well as their relationship with their mother. They are both in their forties and ESTHER lives in England and SILVIE in LA. SILVIE is a flamboyant risk taker but ESTHER has always played by the rules and her mother's revelation has given her a headache. When SILVIE looks for some tablets for ESTHER she finds some long forgotten cocaine in her vanity case, much to ESTHER's horror.

ESTHER/SILVIE

ESTHER: Have you got anything for a headache?

SILVIE: Probably.

> (*She rummages through her vanity case, removes some smelling salts, holds them under ESTHER's nose.*)

> Tom bought them for me. He said they would take away the stale smell. Of the memories, not me. Or maybe he did mean me?

> (*SILVIE removes a variety of things that include bottles of vitamin pills, a shower cap, a bottle of headache pills. She opens the bottle of headache pills and stares, in disbelief. There are no pills, just a small wrap which she removes.*)

> Oh my God. What the hell is this doing in here?

> (*SILVIE offers ESTHER the wrap.*)

ESTHER: Will it clear my head?

SILVIE: Guaranteed to.

> (*SILVIE carefully opens the wrap.*)

ESTHER: Salt?

> (*SILVIE dips her finger into the wrap and rubs the powder into her gums.*)

SILVIE: Waste not want not.

ESTHER: You carried salt all the way over from LA and now you're rubbing it into your gums?

SILVIE: Yeah, I wouldn't want to get cramp. It's cocaine. I carried cocaine all the way over from LA.

ESTHER: Cocaine?

SILVIE: About a quarter of a gram. I didn't know it was still in there. It's good stuff.

> (*SILVIE puts a bit more on her finger, rubs her gums.*)

ESTHER: Are you mad? There are easier ways of putting yourself in prison. Why did you do it?

SILVIE: Oh, you know, adventure.

ESTHER: It's some of your herbal stuff.

SILVIE: It's herbal alright.

ESTHER: I don't believe you.

SILVIE: Want to try some?

ESTHER: No.

SILVIE: Ever tried it?

ESTHER: Why would I?

SILVIE: Why wouldn't you? Don't you go to parties?

ESTHER: Not your kind of parties. I just don't see the point in being out of your face…

SILVIE: Off my face…

ESTHER: Off your head…

SILVIE: Out of my head… This is probably the most dangerous thing I've ever done without knowing it. Want to try some? Go on. One thin little line.

(*ESTHER shakes her head.*

SILVIE handles the wrap with great care.)

Pass me that.

(*SILVIE notices their mother's hand mirror.*

SILVIE empties the contents of the packet onto the mirror.)

ESTHER: What are you doing?

SILVIE: Showing the cocaine how good it looks? You've really never taken any drugs in your life?

ESTHER: Never.

SILVIE: Paracetamol? Aspirin? Anti depressants? Prozac maybe? Weren't you taking Prozac for a while?

ESTHER: It's not the same.

SILVIE: I treat myself occasionally, to a little surprise, a little suggestion of happiness and you think I'm bad?

ESTHER: I didn't say you were bad.

SILVIE: Well you know what? I am bad. And I love every minute of it. When I take this stuff it's because I want to, not because I have to. Get a credit card out of my bag.

ESTHER: A credit card?

SILVIE: Just get it.

ESTHER: Any one in particular?

(*ESTHER opens SILVIE's bag, removes a credit card, gives it to SILVIE.*)

(*SILVIE cuts the cocaine.*)

SILVIE: You really should try some of this. It might loosen you up, unblock some of that anal retention.

ESTHER: I am not anally retentive.

SILVIE: It'll get rid of your headache.

(*ESTHER watches in disgust as SILVIE cuts four long lines, all the time teasing ESTHER.*)

ESTHER: You could have been stopped and put in prison. They might have thought you belonged to some fundamentalist organisation.

SILVIE: So, do you want some?

ESTHER: No.

SILVIE: Just one little snort. One little sniff. Might be your last chance before you get to fifty.

ESTHER: There are plenty of other things I'd like to do before I get to fifty.

SILVIE: Me too.

ESTHER: I thought you'd done it all?

SILVIE: I'd like to learn a language. Maybe Italian. Bongiorno. Mi chiamo Silvie. We have an Italian cleaner. Her eyesight's terrible but she's pretty. You can't have an unattractive cleaner in LA you know. It gives the family a bad name.

ESTHER: Do you do this often?

SILVIE: Only on Fridays and holy days.

(*SILVIE takes a rupee note out of her purse, rolls it up tight.*)

I've never done it with a foreign note before. How exciting.

ESTHER: Do you have to use her mirror?

SILVIE: You want to go first? It won't kill you.

(*ESTHER looks at the cocaine on the mirror.*)

(*SILVIE passes the mirror to her.*)

Wipe some off with your finger and spread it on your gums.

ESTHER: Like Bonjela?

SILVIE: Yes, just like that.

(*ESTHER holds the mirror, looks at the powder.*)

PART TWO
MALE/MALE
DUOLOGUES

From

CROSSFIRE

by Michel Azama (translated by Nigel Gearing)

This translation was first performed by Paines Plough at The Traverse Theatre, Edinburgh, in August 1993.

Crossfire explores how ordinary human beings are caught up in the atrocity of war. YONATHAN and ISMAIL are fifteen years old and have known each other all their lives. They now find themselves pitched against each other in a religious civil war and YONATHAN and his family are forced to move away because they face religious persecution. ISMAIL doesn't understand how YONATHAN could move to the 'other side' and tries to persuade him to stay.

YONATHAN/ISMAIL

YONATHAN: Ismail, I'm going. I mean, I'm not just going, I'm leaving you.

ISMAIL: Where to?

YONATHAN: The other side.

ISMAIL: What. To them others?

YONATHAN: Yes.

ISMAIL: Have you gone mad or what?

YONATHAN: My family's a different religion from yours. We settled here before everything blew up like this. Now it's not the same any more. Our place is over there. Opposite.

ISMAIL: With them others?

YONATHAN: We're part of them others.

ISMAIL: It's crazy. You were born here. We've always played soccer together. It's crazy.

YONATHAN: Absolutely.

ISMAIL: No one will hurt you here. You come from round here.

YONATHAN: Who knows. Things have changed so quickly.

ISMAIL: We're trapped. I feel lost. I try and understand what's going on. I listen to the radio. I try and keep up. This war's a war of lies. Everybody's lying. You can't know any more.

YONATHAN: I've got gut trouble. I'm getting nervous and irritable. I'm sleeping very badly. I can't get to sleep.

ISMAIL: You should count the shells.

YONATHAN: That's what I do. It wakes me up. Ismail, I'm off.

ISMAIL: Wait. You can't leave just like that. We'll still see each other.

YONATHAN: Won't be so easy when we're on opposite sides.

ISMAIL: When we were kids the war was just a good excuse for bunking off school. You remember, we used to say: no school today! Today's a bombing-day!

You can't go off with them.

We're lions and they're just dogs.

YONATHAN: That's how it is. There's nothing we can do about it.

ISMAIL: You're my mate. My mate. One hundred per cent. I can't think of you as the enemy, it's impossible. I'd get killed for you here and now like a shot... Like a shot.

You remember you wanted to be a doctor and me an engineer.

On my fifteenth birthday we had a party, a picnic by the sea with some girls.

There haven't been any since.

YONATHAN: There won't be any more, Ismail.

ISMAIL: Yonathan! We said we'd never split up.

YONATHAN: We were kids. The war hadn't started then. Not really. Not like nowadays.

ISMAIL: Remember, that was the day it began.

YONATHAN: What's the point.

ISMAIL: For our picnic we had a barbecue. We danced with the girls. When we got back we didn't understand what that guy was saying. He was saying things are hotting up out there and when we got back...

YONATHAN: Yes. Usually a bit of a fuss, a bit of a noise then nothing.

I have to go.

Have to be across the line by nightfall.

ISMAIL: I found my mother in tears. She thought I was dead.

YONATHAN: Mine too. You'd flirted with the most beautiful girl. Let's stop this. It's pointless.

ISMAIL: You were jealous.

YONATHAN: That was in peace time. Not the same.

ISMAIL: We've spent our whole lives playing soccer and stealing figs.

YONATHAN: All that's over now.

ISMAIL: You can't leave just like that. Over on the other side with the others. I don't believe you. Shooting at us. Shooting at me perhaps. I can't believe that.

YONATHAN: Whether you believe it or not makes no difference.

I'm sorry we're not the same religion. One day we could have met up again in the same Heaven.

ISMAIL: You haven't a single real feeling in the whole of your body.

YONATHAN: Yes I have.

ISMAIL: What? What feeling? Tell me.

YONATHAN: The feeling that from one side or another everyone's pushing us towards our graves.

ISMAIL: That's no answer. I don't want you to leave.

YONATHAN: I have to. Give us a hug, Ismail.

ISMAIL: No. Piss off.

(*They hug. YONATHAN runs off.*)

Yonathaaaaaaaaan.

Come back. Yonathan. Don't go. Over there they're just dogs and we're lions. Yonathan.

From

TALKIN' LOUD
by Trevor Williams

Talkin' Loud *was first performed at the Latchmere Theatre,*
London (now Theatre 503) in February 2004.

Talkin' Loud explores the choices available for young black men
in our inner cities. JOSHUA and KWAME are twenty-one years old
and live on a London estate. Joshua is studying and exploring
his musical talent – the world seems as though it's at his feet.
However, the stress of being attacked at gunpoint changes
everything for him. This scene looks back to when JOSHUA and
KWAME were seventeen. JOSHUA has found some guns, belonging
to his older brother Carl, and shows one to KWAME.

KWAME/JOSHUA

KWAME: So where yuh get it?

JOSHUA: Carl.

KWAME: Yuh brodda give it to yuh!

JOSHUA: Don't be stupid! My brodda's gonna give me any gun? Found it innit?

KWAME: Where?

JOSHUA: Upstairs rooting out some dollars for the tutor, there it was.

KWAME: What, just lying there, on a pure come hither vibe?

JOSHUA: Na, wrapped up tight, plastic bag, bubble wrap and shit, four of them.

KWAME: Wha?

JOSHUA: Four.

KWAME: Cheez!

JOSHUA: Yeah, that bubble wrap's addictive yuh know. I was popping that shit half an hour at leas'.

KWAME: The others' still there?

JOSHUA: Yeah.

(*KWAME looks at the ceiling.*

Beat before he hands the gun back to JOSHUA.)

KWAME: Yuh bes' put it back before he finds it.

JOSHUA: Yeah.

(*JOSHUA doesn't move.*)

KWAME: Yuh seen one before?

JOSHUA: Yeah.

KWAME: Na, not on telly, real, like life?

JOSHUA: No.

KWAME: Me neither.

(*KWAME looks as if he's thinking something.*)

JOSHUA: What…? I know yuh gonna say summin' now.

KWAME: Na just…first time.

JOSHUA: What?

KWAME: Seeing something like this, for real…

JOSHUA: Yeah…?

KWAME: Blows yuh away innit? Yuh know it but yuh don't really
know it yuh know?

JOSHUA: What!? Know it but don't really know it. That don't make
no sense.

KWAME: Na but it's…like the first time yuh see summin' yuh ain't
seen before, for real, 3D, like a…an animal.

JOSHUA: What?

KWAME: Yeah, like an elephant.

JOSHUA: Elephant!?

KWAME: Na wait, wait. Yuh know when you're a kid how yuh get
obsessed wid stuff?

JOSHUA: No.

KWAME: I did, elephants. Then I saw *The Jungle Book* and that was it.
That scene when the elephants and Mowgli go on parade.

JOSHUA: Wha yuh talking about?

KWAME: Yuh ain't seen it? Yuh gotta see it. There's this scene in the
film when Mowgli, thass the little boy, goes on parade wid the
elephants. It's…I used to wanna watch that bit over and over
touching the screen and everyt'ing. Always on my dad's case to
take me to see one. He said they were in Africa as well, bigger
though, roamin' round, free and easy.

JOSHUA: He probably just said that to shut yuh up.

KWAME: I've gotta go Africa innit?

JOSHUA: Kwame, this is a serious piece of hardware and you're
talking 'bout Africa and…Elephants.

KWAME: Na, but don't yuh think it's strange wid the guns?

JOSHUA: What?

KWAME: Yuh always hearing like they're everywhere, the streets
awash wid them.

JOSHUA: Where?

KWAME: Exactly but everyone expects yuh to have one.

JOSHUA: Everyone who?

KWAME: In the papers and…what we talking about in general studies. Every time they mention estates like this it's gun this, gun that.

JOSHUA: Thass papers innit? Who believes that?

KWAME: People. Go uptown I swear certain man's 'fraid to look in yuh eye in case spark him. Proper scared cos of that power in yuh hand.

JOSHUA: Thass what yuh want, the power.

KWAME: So how comes we ain't seen one before now? And I bet none of them down there ain't neither.

JOSHUA: Let's go show them.

KWAME: Na, na, thass not what I mean. It's about we're meant to have, but we don't have.

JOSHUA: Yeah…?

KWAME: Yeah, so…

JOSHUA: Whass wid yuh today? On that matrix vibe again? Equations mus' be fucking wid your brain one time.

KWAME: But listen, if we don't have and everyone's expecting us to, why not?

JOSHUA: Why not what?

KWAME: Live the life, go out blazing, blingin' it.

JOSHUA: Now yuh talkin'

(*He grabs the gun from JOSHUA and goes to the window looking out. He then moves away again. He feels the weight of it in his hand.*)

KWAME: I bet there some kickback on this.

JOSHUA: Yuh know that.

(*Beat.*)

KWAME: Yuh seen an elephant innit?

JOSHUA: What?

KWAME: Elephant?

JOSHUA: Course.

KWAME: Zoo?

JOSHUA: Where else?

KWAME: Yeah. It ain't the same as seeing it in the wild though. Imagine that.

From

PLAYING FIELDS
by Neela Dolezalova

Playing Fields *was first performed at Soho Theatre, London in October 2002.*

JUSTIN is sixteen years old and has just learnt that he is going to be a father. He was with Thyme only one night and was too scared to return her calls. Thyme is now pregnant and in a relationship with Felicity (Flea) and wants nothing more to do with him. The two girls have been busy fighting for the survival of the local playing fields in North London. Thyme tells JUSTIN that she is pregnant at her cousin PETE's flat when JUSTIN turns up unexpectedly. PETE is eighteen years old and although he is Thyme's cousin they were brought up like brother and sister. Thyme baits JUSTIN a little and likens him to the playing fields, which need saving just as much as he does (JUSTIN's father used to beat him). Thyme leaves and JUSTIN is faced with explaining himself to PETE.

/ denotes the point of interruption by the following character.

PETE/JUSTIN

PETE: Did you rape her? Is that what it was? Did you / Justin?

JUSTIN: (*Sarcasm.*) Yeah, that's right. Couldn't help myself Pete. Looked like she deserved it, it weren't my fault, she was asking / for it.

PETE: You think you're a soldier, don't you? You dirty little / fucker

JUSTIN: It was done out of mutual respect. / For fuck's sake Pete.

PETE: Oh, what? So she agreed did she?

JUSTIN: You won't believe me will you?

PETE: What do you expect?

JUSTIN: Well she more than agreed. Little slag couldn't get enough.

PETE: How could you?

JUSTIN: It weren't just me Pete.

PETE: I wish it were. Should have kept your germs to your fucking self.

JUSTIN: Where's this going Pete? What do you want from me? Cos I won't even hit ya Pete. I'll just close my eyes, and think 'bout what I done.

PETE: What?

JUSTIN: I don't want to fight you, Pete. I couldn't take that. But I understand why you'd feel that about me. If I were you, I'd have kicked the shit out of me already.

PETE: Yeah, cos that would be fucking great. Pregnant schoolgirl with father in intensive care. Yeah great, that's the best thing you've come up with all night. What do you think I am?

JUSTIN: So you're not going to fight me?

PETE: No.

(*Pause. Calmer.*)

JUSTIN: I would've.

PETE: Yeah?

(*Pause. JUSTIN sits down.*)

How far gone is she Justin?

JUSTIN: Don't know.

PETE: So it happened more than once did it?

JUSTIN: No.

PETE: Then when was it?

JUSTIN: Before summer.

PETE: Before? Before when? For fuck's sake / give a proper date.

JUSTIN: June. Beginning. I don't know.

PETE: Justin /

JUSTIN: Yeah, the first week of June.

> (*Pause.*)

PETE: Do you love her?

JUSTIN: What?

PETE: Do you love her?

> (*Pause. JUSTIN nods.*)
>
> What was that?

JUSTIN: Yes. Yes I did.

PETE: Did?

JUSTIN: I felt for her. Yeah, I did Pete. I felt for that girl, you don't / understand

PETE: Then what happened? How come's she couldn't tell ya?

JUSTIN: She wanted to.

PETE: (*Getting angry again.*) What?

JUSTIN: I never spoke to her when she rang.

PETE: Why not?

JUSTIN: Cos it hurt.

PETE: What hurt? Hurt more than finding out you're pregnant? Huh?

JUSTIN: It hurt cos I knew she didn't feel for me. That's why. Yeah, fuck, I'm someone special, but at the end of the day she loves Flea don't she? I knew that Pete. What do you want a man to do? Keep hassling her? I was just a thing for her. Something out the past to finish. Closure.

PETE: I don't believe you.

JUSTIN: Then don't.

PETE: It only happened once yeah?

JUSTIN: Yeah.

PETE: Why didn't you tell me?

JUSTIN: Cos I knew you'd screw. She weren't my territory.

PETE: Territory?

JUSTIN: League.

PETE: Oh, you've really got a way with words you have. What an idiot.

(*Pause.*)

After so many years you didn't even feel like you had the opportunity to tell me in some way. Both of you. I wouldn't have been angry about the relationship. Why deceive, omit the truth?

JUSTIN: What?

PETE: Omission Justin.

JUSTIN: What does that mean?

PETE: You hid the truth from me. You *chose* not to tell me.

JUSTIN: She hid the truth from me.

PETE: So every time I've seen you since school, every draw we've shared, whatever yeah, you've been looking at me and thinking what an idiot I am. That you've slept with my sister. Behind my back 'n all. Jesus. How could you step into this house? You're some brave mother-fucker. I rate you.

JUSTIN: It was only once. It weren't going anywhere.

PETE: It's gone too far.

JUSTIN: Yeah well. It's only three months. She can get it sucked out or summin.

PETE: Excuse me?

JUSTIN: Bitch can go get it sucked out. She's not keeping it.

PETE: Who are you to say that?

JUSTIN: The little fucker's father apparently.

PETE: I didn't just hear you say that.

JUSTIN: Yeah? She can come back another day when she knows what being a fucking father means. Then I'll get her proper shafted. She'll be dropping little brats in every fucking Mothercare she goes to.

(*PETE hits him.*)

Shit Thyme. You don't even know what you've done. You just broke my world.

From

HARVEST
by Richard Bean

*The first performance was at The Royal Court's Jerwood
Theatre, London in September 2005.*

In 1875, Lord Primrose Agar, wagered eighty-two acres of his
land in East Yorkshire that his dog would outlive one of his tenant
farmers, ninety-four year old Orlando Harrison. Thirteen years
later the dog died and Orlando became a landowner. *Harvest*
is the story of the Harrison family's continual struggle to keep
hold of the land. The play starts in 1914 after Orlando's death
and his two descendants, WILLIAM and ALBERT, argue over who
should go to war and who should stay at home to look after the
farm. WILLIAM is described as nineteen years old and handsome
with refined features. ALBERT is described as eighteen and
broader and rougher. The scene is set around the big farmhouse
table mid-morning.

WILLIAM/ALBERT

WILLIAM: 'ot.

ALBERT: Aye

    (*WILLIAM quenches his thirst using a cup.*)

    Where d'yer go on yer 'lowance?

WILLIAM: Mind yer own.

ALBERT: Spittle Garth meadow?

WILLIAM: Mebbe. Mebbe not.

    (*WILLIAM pours some stew from a pot, cuts some bread, sits and begins to eat.*)

ALBERT: He found out worr it was.

WILLIAM: Aye?

ALBERT: Aye.

    (*ALBERT runs wet hands through his hair, and spits noisily into the sink. He ladles himself some stew, cuts some bread, sits and starts to eat. WILLIAM looks to ALBERT for further enlightenment but gets none.*)

WILLIAM: What worr it?

ALBERT: A vixen.

WILLIAM: Aye?

ALBERT: Aye.

WILLIAM: I said it worr a fox all along. I said to him, I said, 'That's the work of either one of two beasts. A fox or a Bengal Tiger.'

ALBERT: Aye?

WILLIAM: Aye. D'he kill it?

ALBERT: Aye.

WILLIAM: Good.

ALBERT: They say the Kaiser's gorr a withered arm.

WILLIAM: 'They say.'

ALBERT: His left arm. He can't even shek hands with it.

WILLIAM: No-one sheks wi' the left hand. Norr even kings.

ALBERT: They've given him a little cane to carry. So he's gorr an excuse not to have to use it.

WILLIAM: (*Impersonating the Kaiser.*) 'I vud like to help you lift zat barrel but vat vud I do vid ze cane.'

(*Pause. They eat.*)

The problem we've gorr is that we both wanna go. But we can't both go. Worr I'm saying is we have to find a way of deciding who's gooin. Me or you.

ALBERT: Dad's dead.

WILLIAM: I had noticed.

ALBERT: I'm the youngest. Eldest son gets the farm. You get the farm, so you stay. All around here it's the youngest what is gooin. Sid's gooin.

WILLIAM: Mad Sid or Little Sid?

ALBERT: They wouldn't have Mad Sid.

WILLIAM: What's wrong with Mad Sid?

ALBERT: Teeth.

WILLIAM: Aye, he's got terrible teeth. I didn't know they was choosey. So Little Sid's gooin is he?

ALBERT: Aye. He's learning hissen some French. For the girls. They eat a lot of red meat don't they, French girls. They say it meks 'em alles ready for loving.

WILLIAM: Little Sid's an expert on French women is he? Every day he drives a cart from Driffield to Beverley and back again. When he gets adventurous, when he wakes up in the morning and thinks he's Captain Fucking Cook, he goes as far as Hull.

ALBERT: We could have a fight.

WILLIAM: You'd win. Look, you're good with the 'osses. Most things I do, mam can do, but she don't like the 'osses over much.

ALBERT: They're onny 'osses, you don't have to like 'em. You like Brandy.

WILLIAM: Brandy's a beautiful good natured 'oss. I an't gorr a problem with her. It's the others.

ALBERT: So what yer saying? I stay and work the farm cos I'm good with 'osses and keep it gooin so you can goo off to France and have yer fun and when you come back yer can tek it over again beein as you's the auldest.

WILLIAM: You mek it sound like summat scheming. I don't see the justice in me missing out on gooin ovverseas just cos I'm twelve month aulder 'an you.

ALBERT: Worrabout your project?

WILLIAM: This war'll all be over well afore the spring and spring is the right time for me project.

ALBERT: Why won't yer tell no-one worr it is?

WILLIAM: Cos it's a bloody secret project.

ALBERT: Go on, tell us.

WILLIAM: No, I'm not telling yer.

ALBERT: It's pigs innit?

WILLIAM: Who towld yer?

ALBERT: Mam. I don't like pigs.

WILLIAM: Pigs is onny mathematics. Yer not saying, 'I don't like pigs', yer saying, 'I don't like mathematics.'

ALBERT: As I see it, we both wanna go, so – [we both go and –]

WILLIAM: – we're gooin round the houses here.

(*Pause.*)

Did you book the stallion man?

ALBERT: Aye. He's on his way through to Langtoft. He's staying there tonight. Should be here soon.

WILLIAM: Where'd he stay last night?

ALBERT: Rudston.

WILLIAM: Different bed every night eh. You'd like that would yer?

ALBERT: Aye. They say the stallion man has fun in about equal measure to that stallion of his. They say he's fathered –

WILLIAM: – 'They say.' Who are these they?

ALBERT: You should see his clothes. He's all rigged out for the music hall. Breeches, yellow waistcoat, bowler hat. Like a bloody Lord. Cane with a brass knob on the end.

WILLIAM: Aye, well we all know what that's for.

ALBERT: (*Laughing.*) Aye.

WILLIAM: He's a nobody. He's gorr a big 'oss and the gift of the gab. Any fool could be a stallion man. You could be a stallion man.

ALBERT: Oh now – [come on it ain't that easy]

WILLIAM: – Get yersen a big 'oss and a fancy hat. You're good with 'osses. Then you'd get yer travel. Different bed every night.

ALBERT: To be a proper stallion man you godda have summat…I dunno…summat –

WILLIAM: – indefinable.

ALBERT: Aye.

WILLIAM: Personality.

ALBERT: Aye.

WILLIAM: Well you an't got that.

(*Beat.*) Will Brandy stand for that stallion of his?

ALBERT: Aye, she's 'ot. Should be a beautiful 'oss out of our Brandy and that big Percheron of his. Pedigree.

(*ALBERT finishes his stew and licks the plate. He then lights his pipe. WILLIAM finishes his stew, cuts himself a piece of bread and wipes his plate with the bread and eats it.*)

Bit fancy.

WILLIAM: I'm courting ain't I.

ALBERT: Aye, you've been behaving summat a long way off the regular all harvest.

WILLIAM: That'll be the courting.

ALBERT: (*After a decent draw on his pipe.*) I 'ad me eye on Maudie.

WILLIAM: We bin through this afore.

ALBERT: I thought you might go for that sister of hers.

WILLIAM: I like Maudie. Kate's a bit of an 'andful. Why don't yer have a try at Kate?

ALBERT: (*Knowing he's no chance.*) Oh aye.

(*WILLIAM lights a cigarette.*)

If you're courting Maudie, you'd berrer stay, and I'll go.

WILLIAM: We've onny just started courting.

ALBERT: (*Standing.*) I'm not courting no-one at all. That's all I'm saying. You are. And I'm the youngest. Everywhere round here it's the youngest what is gooin.

From

WHO'S BREAKING?
by Philip Osment

Who's Breaking? *was first performed in September 1989*
by Red Ladder Theatre Company.

STEVE is in his late teens and HIV positive (after sharing
needles down at the local gym where he was injecting anabolic
steroids). He's forced to re-think his life, as well as his attitudes
towards homosexuals with whom he has to spend time at the
AIDS Advice Centre. In this scene, STEVE turns up early for
his first 'body positive meeting' at the centre. He meets CHRIS,
a volunteer in his early twenties. CHRIS scares STEVE away by
(wrongly) assuming he is gay like himself.

CHRIS/STEVE

CHRIS: Hello.

STEVE: Hello.

CHRIS: You come for the body positive meeting?

STEVE: Err, yeah.

CHRIS: No one else is here yet. I don't think people start arriving till half past.

STEVE: Oh, I see.

CHRIS: My name's Chris. I'm learning how to be a volunteer.

STEVE: I'm Steve.

CHRIS: Steve. Right. Do you want a drink? There's no coffee because the urn hasn't boiled but they've got apple juice, pineapple juice, no orange, tropical fruit or Perrier – well, it's not Perrier, but it's the same thing only cheaper.

STEVE: Oh, yeah.

CHRIS: Which?

STEVE: Orange.

CHRIS: No, they haven't got any orange.

STEVE: Oh, err, apple.

CHRIS: Right.

(He gets STEVE a plastic cup of juice.)

Did you have far to come?

STEVE: Quite a way. I live over in Endsley.

CHRIS: Here. *(He hands him the drink.)*

STEVE: Ta.

CHRIS: That's not very far. Only take five minutes in the car.

STEVE: I walked.

CHRIS: You live on your own?

STEVE: No, with me Mam and Dad.

CHRIS: Must be awkward.

(Pause.)

This your first time, then?

STEVE: I only had the result of me test the other week.

CHRIS: How you coping?

STEVE: Okay, like. It's difficult to grasp really.

CHRIS: Yeah.

STEVE: Don't think it's sunk in.

CHRIS: Must take time to adjust. Talking to other people who are going through the same thing will help.

STEVE: What happens at these meetings?

CHRIS: Well, last week was my first week. They spent the first half talking about business – you know, finances, fundraising, arranging meetings with other groups in the area. Then they had a talk on alternative medicine.

STEVE: What's that?

CHRIS: The speaker was a homeopath.

STEVE: Lot of it about isn't there?

(*They both laugh.*)

CHRIS: Then they split up into small groups.

STEVE: What for?

CHRIS: To talk.

STEVE: What do they talk about?

CHRIS: Depends. Things like, you know, anger. Lot of people feel very angry.

STEVE: When I heard about the bloke I got it off I felt sorry for him. Then when I got me result I wanted to kill him.

CHRIS: Mmmmm.

STEVE: I only went round with him for about six months.

CHRIS: Do your Mam and Dad know about you and him?

STEVE: No, me Dad would kill me.

CHRIS: Yeah, well, when I told my parents, my Dad said to me I'd rather you were dead.

STEVE: When did you tell them?

CHRIS: Ages ago.

STEVE: How long have you known?

CHRIS: Since I was twelve.

STEVE: Hey?

CHRIS: I've got one mate who says he knew he was gay when he was six. It's not fair is it? It's hard enough growing up gay in a straight world without all those bastards saying what we do is evil and AIDS is the punishment for it. I'd be more than angry if I was body positive. I mean it makes you want to kill, doesn't it?

STEVE: Errr – yeah.

CHRIS: I mean that's why they have this gay men's group tonight. So we can all bitch about straights.

(*Pause.*)

I don't mean that. Some of my best friends are straight.

(*He laughs.*)

You got many straight friends?

STEVE: Yeah.

CHRIS: Last week someone said we shouldn't have anything to do with the straight people who use the centre. I don't agree with that, though. I know straight men can be really boring but they can't help it. Sometimes they even say something sensible. Do you want another apple juice?

STEVE: Uhhh, no... I err... I just remembered... I've got to go.

CHRIS: You what?

STEVE: I'm meeting somebody. I forgot.

CHRIS: Can't you rearrange it? You can use the phone if you want.

STEVE: No, it's alright.

CHRIS: You sure?

STEVE: Yeah.

CHRIS: Well, come back later. We'll be here till ten.

STEVE: Yeah, right, I will. Bye.

CHRIS: Bye.

(*STEVE goes.*

CHRIS stands looking puzzled. Slowly his mistake starts to dawn on him.)

(*Under his breath.*) Shit.

From

MONSTER
by Duncan Macmillan

Monster won *Second Prize in the Bruntwood Playwriting
Competition for the Royal Exchange, part of the Manchester
International Festival, and was first performed at the Royal
Exchange Theatre, Manchester, in June 2007.*

TOM is an inexperienced trainee teacher in his thirties who has
been employed to work with DARRYL, a violent and disturbed
fourteen year old boy, who has been taken out of lessons and
is facing permanent exclusion. They come from completely
different backgrounds: DARRYL is white and is being brought
up by his Nan because his mother committed suicide when
high on drugs, whilst TOM is black, was brought up in Surrey
and is not very street-wise. This scene is taken from their first
meeting and they are alone in a classroom.

TOM/DARRYL

TOM: Darryl, do you understand why you've been taken out of lessons?

Darryl?

,

DARRYL: Yes.

TOM: Why?

DARRYL: 'Cause Head of Year's a bitch init?

TOM: No.

DARRYL: Beyatch.

TOM: No.

DARRYL: Wants a smack.

TOM: Darryl

DARRYL: Godzilla.

TOM: Now,

DARRYL: she come up in here now I'd box her down. I'd be like, 'hey, Miss, man, eat this bitch' and she'd be like 'noooo' and I'd be like 'booosch!' like that thing that thing have you seen it, that thing that video mobile

TOM: Darryl,

DARRYL: that 'Happy Slappers'.

TOM: Darryl we don't refer to it as that in this school.

DARRYL: It's wicked.

TOM: What do we refer to it as?

DARRYL: Fucking excellent.

TOM: Common assault.

DARRYL: Oh yeah, yeah, Common assault yeah. Video the common assault on your mobile and send it everyone. It's slammin'

TOM: Darryl, three students have been excluded this year for

DARRYL: there's this one, yeah, where they get this girl in a headlock, yeah, they hold her so she can't move and then 'bout ten a these guys

TOM: I don't want to hear about that Darryl. I'm not impressed by that.

DARRYL: I got Saddam. What's your number? I'll text it you.

TOM: Will you put that away?

DARRYL: You got Bluetooth?

TOM: Put your phone away.

DARRYL: Have you though?

TOM: Sit properly please Darryl.

DARRYL: Bet you got an old dinosaur phone init? Big cream-coloured brick with antennae and shit.

TOM: Sit on your chair properly please.

DARRYL: Like your crepes init?

TOM: My what?

DARRYL: Your shoes.

'

TOM: What about my shoes?

DARRYL: They're shit.

Sorry, but they is.

They're wack.

You gived them an ikkle bit a scrub and t'ing, polish dem up an' that. But dey still cheap init? Laces don't match. New laces. Old shoes. You had dem for *time*.

TOM: You're very observant Darryl.

DARRYL: True dat. Keep my eyes open init?

TOM: I'm impressed.

DARRYL: Can I axe you a question?

TOM: Darryl,

DARRYL: can I though?

TOM: No. Not right now.

DARRYL: Gosh man. Just want to arks a question init?

'

(*TOM sits down.*)

TOM: What do you want to know?

DARRYL: What would you do, yeah, if you were on a plane and someone was like 'you're all gonna die, I'm gonna fly this bitch into a wall'?

TOM: Darryl, why don't we look at the

DARRYL: would you be scared?

TOM: Darryl, come on let's

DARRYL: would you though? I bet you would.

I bet you'd shit yourself.

TOM: Darryl, alright, listen,

DARRYL: did you go to this school?

TOM: No, I

I went to school in Surrey.

DARRYL: Is it?

TOM: Yes.

DARRYL: Why?

(*DARRYL has taken a lighter from his pocket.*)

TOM: Because that's where I lived.

Will you sit on your chair properly Darryl?

DARRYL: Well posh init? Surrey?

TOM: Not really.

(*DARRYL ignites the lighter.*)

Darryl give me that. You know the rules.

(*DARRYL runs a finger through the flame.*)

DARRYL: Can I ask you a question?

TOM: Give that to me. Now.

DARRYL: Why?

TOM: Because of fire regulations.

DARRYL: I'm not gonna burn the school down.

TOM: Just give it to me please.

'

DARRYL: Alright.

(*DARRYL pushes the lighter across the table. TOM reaches over, takes it and puts it in his pocket.*)

TOM: Tell me how you feel your lessons have been going.

From

CAR
by Chris O'Connell

*Car was first performed by Theatre Absolute, in co-production
with the Belgrade Theatre, on 22 June 1999, in Coventry's
Transport Museum. The play transferred to the Pleasance
Theatre for the 1999 Edinburgh Festival and won the
Scotsman Fringe First Award for outstanding new work.
After transferring to the Pleasance Theatre, London, Car was
awarded a Time Out Live Award – Best New Play on the
London Fringe, 1999.*

The play opens with the theft of a car by four boys where the
owner is violently injured. One of the boys, NICK (in his early
twenties) feels guilty about what's happened and approaches
his probation officer, ROB (in his forties) with the situation.
They meet in ROB's office.

The symbol / indicates an interruption point.

NICK/ROB

(*NICK faces ROB and stirs, as if from deep in thought.*)

NICK: …what?

ROB: I said…

NICK: What?

ROB: I said, 'It's always nice to see you, but is this just a social visit cos there's no one else to knock around with, or did you come up to see me for a specific reason?'

(*No answer.*)

So what's up?

NICK: Nothing.

(*ROBERT waits.*)

What?

ROB: I'm waiting.

NICK: Don't look at your watch, yeah?

ROB: I'm not. I just wasn't expecting you, it's not a supervision day is it.

(*Pause.*)

You in the shit again?

NICK: Something like that.

(*ROBERT sighs.*)

That's exactly why I wasn't going to come.

ROB: What is?

NICK: *That*, you sighing, acting like I'm some fucking useless…

ROB: Well what did you think I was going to say? You've been told enough times haven't you, you know what *is* and what *isn't* against the law.

NICK: I know that yeah, you don't need to go on and stuff.

ROB: So what happened?

NICK: Don't know, just one of them yeah?

(*Pause.*)

ROB: Look, I was sighing because I wish you'd just come up here and like…just pass the time of day or something, but it's always got to be when you've gone and fucked up somewhere.

NICK: You're swearing now yeah?

(*ROBERT glares at him. Softens.*)

ROB: I'm just racked off, you've been doing alright. (*Pause.*) So what is it, what you been up to?

NICK: I didn't mean it…yeah?

(*Beat.*)

ROB: Didn't mean what?

(*No answer.*)

Didn't mean what?

NICK: …Me and these others…we robbed this bloke's car. Most times stuff like that goes in one ear, and out the other. But then there's this car, and everything gets fucked up…the bloke starts chasing us and he ends up on the roof…he's smashed up on the road and the other guys they just…and I'm fucking… It's doing my fucking head in…going round, night time, day time, what we did to that guy… And it's like, how bad do I get yeah?

ROB: Bad?

NICK: All the years, all the badness I'm storing up and now it's coming out.

ROB: Nick, you've been a bit of an idiot, / you've done some stupid things, but…

NICK: I *know* what I'm like yeah, fucking dam builder man.

(*Pause.*)

ROB: You could get sent down for this, you know?

NICK: Got to hand myself in first.

ROB: Well don't start thinking it's going to go / away.

NICK: Yeah.

ROB: What if you were able to meet up with this bloke?

NICK: Who?

ROB: The one whose motor you nicked?

(*NICK looks at ROBERT like he's just farted.*)

It's just a thought.

NICK: Try another one yeah?!

ROB: Mediation.

NICK: ?

ROB: Bringing the offender and the victim together.

NICK: What?

ROB: You'll be face to face, see what he's feeling, see the effect you've had on him. You'll be able to say sorry to him. Sounds to me that's what you're after.

NICK: So he didn't die then?

ROB: I don't know, did you check the hospitals?

NICK: No.

ROB: Well, I haven't heard anything. Listen, if you do this…

NICK: Do what? I don't know what the fuck all this / mediation shit is…

ROB: I can go through it with you. If you do it then you've got to use it, do you know what I'm saying? Help yourself, make the switch… You're running out of time, every time you let people down, every time you let me down…

NICK: *You?* How am I letting you down? I don't owe you nothing. (*Sees ROBERT's look.*) You think we're mates or something yeah?

(*Pause.*)

ROB: No.

NICK: No. You're my probation officer yeah?

(*ROBERT gets busy, papers, pens etc.*)

ROB: Right, well whatever you decide to do, I'll do what I can to help. Alright?

NICK: You telling me to go?

ROB: Yeah. Seems like you've got the situation sussed, I'm sure you'll sort something out.

NICK: Rob…fuck's sake, you're getting like you're my missus or something, are we having a row yeah?… Don't blank me man!

ROB: You think I'm sitting here for the good of my own health?

NICK: Dunno.

ROB: Don't be a smart arse. You want me to help you, then alright, I'll give you a hundred per cent, but if you / start fucking me about, then…

NICK: It's pressure, fucking pressure all the time yeah?!… I don't want to keep fucking things up… Listen, tell me what this mediation shit's about then, you think it's going to help me…?

ROB: You need to *listen* to what I tell you.

NICK: I am…I will.

(*Beat.*)

ROB: First things first, you better go and hand yourself in.

From

BURNING BLUE
by DMW Greer

Burning Blue *was first produced on London's Fringe at The King's Head Theatre in Islington in March 1995.*

Burning Blue centres around four friends in their early thirties who are top US navy fighter pilots and share an ambition to make it onto the NASA space programme. DAN and WILL are close because of having bailed out of an aircraft after a flock of birds hit them, just before they became fully fledged pilots. However, it is DAN and Matt who develop feelings for each other and are seen dancing together in a gay nightclub in Hong Kong. The incident leads to a full scale investigation by naval intelligence, because of the ban on gays in the US military, and sets in motion a homosexual witch hunt. This strains the friendship between DAN and WILL.

The following duologue occurs at the start of the play, five years prior to the homosexual investigation, when DAN and WILL have just bailed out of their aircraft in parachutes. We see DAN first of all, trying to disentangle himself from his torso harness. WILL is completely covered by his parachute.

DAN/WILL

DAN: Wilbur? Wilbur!

(*We hear coughing as a panicked WILL gasps for air. DAN continues to struggle with his harness so he can get to his buddy.*)

WILL: Dano… I can't breathe… I can't breathe! Dano?! Danoooooo!

(*At last freeing himself, DANO rushes offstage into the water and pulls WILL the short distance to shore. He frees his head from the parachute and we see his face covered in blood. DAN tries to calm him as WILL continues to panic.*)

Oh, God! Oh, my God! I'm bleeding… I'm bleeding!

DAN: You're fine, buddy. You're doing fine…

WILL: Where am I bleeding from?!

DAN: I told you, Will, you're okay!

WILL: My legs! I lost one of my legs, didn't I?!

DAN: Just calm down, Wilbur! You're gonna be fine!

WILL: (*Looking at his hands.*) Mother fuck…my brains…my brains are all over my hands!!

DAN: (*Shaking him.*) Just shut up for a minute! You've got to calm down and listen to me! A bird came through the canopy and hit you in the face. It's bird blood and bird guts.

WILL: Birds? I didn't see any birds…where are we, Dano?!

DAN: Somewhere on the shore of Pensacola Bay.

WILL: I'm freezing…

DAN: Take nice easy breaths and relax.

WILL: I'm so cold.

DAN: (*Cupping his hands for him.*) Here, blow into your hands…

WILL: I thought I was drowning… I thought I was gonna go straight to the bottom.

DAN: You were only ten feet from the shore you wouldn't have drowned in three feet of water…no way.

(*DAN wipes the blood off WILL's hands and then takes hold of his feet.*)

WILL: Aghhhh! Jesus, that hurts! What are you doing?

DAN: I'm gonna get you warm by blowing on your feet. Now just lie back and concentrate on breathing slowly.

WILL: Go easy! I think my ankle's broken.

DAN: Nah… (*Looking at it suspiciously.*) It's probably just a bad sprain.

WILL: What about you, Dano, are you okay?

DAN: I'm fine, buddy, just lie back and take it easy.

(*WILL lies back partially while DAN bandages his ankle.*)

WILL: (*Anguished.*) It's over…it's over…my career's over. A week away from getting our wings and I went and fucked us both!

DAN: It's not over! A bird strike can happen to anybody.

WILL: (*Sitting up and clutching DAN's chest.*) Dano – I… I forgot to lock my visor down…the clouds came in and it got dark so fast – I couldn't see – so I raised my helmet visor and… I broke the regs! What if they find out I was flying with my visor up?

DAN: They won't. Don't worry…

WILL: But there's gonna be an Accident Investigation! I'm fucked… completely fucked!

(*WILL breaks down. After a beat, DAN gets up and smashes his own helmet visor.*)

WILL: What are you doing?

DAN: From now on I had command of the plane! The story is…we landed at one of the abandoned fields and… I moved into the front seat. We took off and…the birds came through the canopy shattering my visor and then we ejected. Got it?

WILL: But what if they find my helmet in the bay? They're gonna know I didn't have my visor secured down.

DAN: Just – just tell 'em you raised it after you hit the water.

WILL: If we lie and they find out we're both history!

DAN: What are you gonna do if you can't fly? Sell widgets in Omaha? No way! We've come too far! We're *both* getting our wings next week, Wilbur! We started together and that's the way we're gonna finish!

(*DAN wraps WILL's feet in the parachute and goes back to WILL and cradles him.*)

WILL: I just scuttled a twenty million dollar aircraft…

DAN: No way, that airframe was a piece of junk! I'm surprised the seats fired.

(*They huddle up together and are quiet for a few beats. DAN begins to laugh.*)

WILL: What's so freakin' funny?

DAN: (*He rubs his butt.*) Nothing like a rocket under your ass to shake up your world. (*He's quiet for a moment and then begins to laugh again.*) We must've looked like a couple of Roman Candles up there!

WILL: I don't find this humorous, Dano, pilots with accidents on their records aren't selected for NASA…this is serious shit! Your dad is gonna have your balls.

(*DAN hates hearing this.*)

DAN: A flock of birds fouled the engine! What could we do!? Whether your visor was up or down doesn't change the fact that we had to abandon the aircraft! And you! You initiated a text-book ejection!

WILL: Me? You mean you.

DAN: No. *You*…remember? Hell, they'll probably give you a medal!

(*WILL looks at DAN and suddenly freezes.*)

What? What is it?

(*WILL leans forward tentatively and wipes what looks like a bloody gash near DAN's eye.*)

WILL: (*He pretends to taste his finger.*) … Gooney Bird.

(*DAN pushes him playfully and they fall in a heap laughing wildly.*)

Our aircraft is a junk heap at the bottom of the Mobile Bay…but we made it! We got out! Cuz we're shit-hot!

DAN: Damn straight! (*He hugs WILL.*) We're alive! So… fuck 'em!

WILL: Yeah! Fuck 'em if they can't take a joke!!!

From

INCARCERATOR
by Torben Betts

Incarcerator *was first performed at The White Bear Theatre,
London in September 1999.*

Written in rhyming couplets, which drive the drama forward to
its bloody end, *Incarcerator* explores the lives of characters who
find themselves trapped by their needs, wants and desires. In
this duologue, JESSOP is getting ready for his marriage to SMITH
and is in a state of panic as he changes into his wedding suit.
MORRIS is his best man and is watching him, lager in hand.

MORRIS/JESSOP

MORRIS: I tell ya, sunshine…fucking chill!

   You need to…

JESSOP: Fuck!

MORRIS: …calm down!

JESSOP: I will!

MORRIS: Your freedom's fucked but no-one's dead!

   No problem then!

JESSOP: Inside my head

   It feels like twenty voices scream:

   'Wake up, ya cunt! Don't live the dream!'

   I'm sweatin', mate! I'm shittin' rocks!

MORRIS: So cancel it!

JESSOP: Just…pass my socks!

MORRIS: A ring, a church, all blessed by God…

JESSOP: What time is it?

MORRIS: A firing squad

   Would shake a man up less than this!

JESSOP: I'm just going for me umpteenth piss…

MORRIS: You infant!

JESSOP: (*Leaving.*)   And so off I fuck!

MORRIS: I see the serpent Marriage suck

   The joyful juices from his heart,

   Now Cupid's loathsome, toxic dart

   Has pierced his breast, his youth is spent,

   Oblivious to Love's intent,

   Says 'Matrimony, bind these hands!

   I'll live a drudge to your demands!

   Shackle me! Denude my hopes!

   Tether me with mawkish ropes!

Take my horizons, shrink them, please,

Into one room! You must appease

This selfless yearning for castration!

For servitude, emasculation!

For days of toil and nights of tension

…and saving up for that extension.'

This wretched tool, this creeping toad…

JESSOP: (*Entering.*) My bladder burns, but nothing's flowed.

MORRIS: Look, where's the father of the bride?

His shotgun's where?

JESSOP: The cab's outside!

MORRIS: Now listen, pal…just pause for breath

And think!

JESSOP: O, fuck!

MORRIS: It seems like Death

Has gripped you by the greasy nuts

And sapped you of your blood and guts

And now…

JESSOP: O, fuck! I hardly know her!

Who is she? Fuck!

MORRIS: Just take it slower!

It's just a day. A piece of paper.

Think of it as just…a caper.

A social custom, etiquette.

S'all bollocks, mate.

JESSOP: I'm deep in debt:

She's made me fork out seven grand!

Her daddy's skint!

MORRIS: Don't understand…

JESSOP: For string quartets, egg mayonnaise,

For salmon (smoked) and canapés,

For champagne, wine (both red and white)

And evening nosh by candlelight,

Some arsehole with his discotheque...

MORRIS: (*Offering beer.*) Look, have a...

JESSOP: (*Accepting.*)   I'm a nervous wreck.

MORRIS: You've borrowed from the bank more cash?

For fuck's sake!

JESSOP: Was a little rash!

You've got to help me...

MORRIS: No can do...

I bailed you...

JESSOP: I depend on you.

MORRIS: I lend you money every year!

You owe...

JESSOP: Fuck me... I've got the fear.

I promised her...

MORRIS: Just calm yourself!

It's detrimental to the health

Is all this stress!

JESSOP: I've...

MORRIS: Take control!

JESSOP: There's more fulfilment on the dole!

MORRIS: Just stop! Now think! What's happened mate?

You've changed, my son. You've changed of late.

Where has he gone, that carefree cub,

The life and soul of bar and club?

Who'd break girls' hearts with just a smile,

Who celebrated life? And while

We other bastards sweated, schemed,

You glided through your days? It seemed

That God, his angels, Jesus Christ

All wanted sex with you. Now, spliced,

My friend, all that must stop.

Some female's plucked you from the shop.

Now, calm. That's it. Yes, have a breather.

Those days are gone.

JESSOP: I won't deceive her!

MORRIS: Of course you won't. And nor you should.

JESSOP: I love!

MORRIS: I know…but weren't it good

When, minted up, we'd prowl the night,

And sniff out kicks and such delight

As this rank place affords a lad?

Those were the best days that we had:

Like hawks, we'd first survey the scene,

We'd pounce and then we'd reconvene

Next morning and discuss our kills,

Comparing notes.

JESSOP: Sad, childish thrills!

There comes a time for that to cease:

The loveless fuck, the girl as piece

Of passive flesh, the drunken spiel,

That spurting out of pain. I feel,

That now with her… It's more, it's love…

It's something I've been dreaming of

Since I was just a kid. No more

Foul fumblings on the floor,

No more cold nights on strangers' rugs,

And fake emotions fuelled by drugs,

No more false laughter, smiling, nodding

Just to get my desperate rod in!

I'm moving on, Stu. Moving out.

I'm growing up.

MORRIS: (*Aside.*) Just, hear him spout

That age-old lie, that lame excuse…

JESSOP: I'll put my life to better use!

MORRIS: Forget the debt then, seize the day.

You'd kill for her…?

JESSOP: O, I would slay

The man who dared to breathe

Unwholesome air on her! Unsheathe

My sword of honour, flashing keen,

Then hack the heart from out the fiend

Who'd threaten her with eyes of lust,

First slice his belly, then I'd bust

His teeth and gums, tear out his tongue,

I'd rupture kidney, puncture lung,

I'd gouge my eyes out with a skewer,

I'd drink the contents of a sewer,

I'd set my flesh and bone on fire,

Unclothed, I'd crawl across barbed wire,

I'd trample babies, OAPs

To place a plaster on her knees!

For her, I'd swallow powdered glass…

MORRIS: (*Aside.*) Perhaps he'd take one up the arse.

JESSOP: Her breasts could launch a thousand ships!

Her body! Christ, she does these strips,

These shows for me…they drive me wild,

She does the nurse, the nun, the child,

She does these voices, dresses up,

She dances just like this. I cup

A tit like this, our groins like so…

We fuck ourselves unconscious. O,
It's ecstasy, it's drugs, it's death!
I smell destruction on her breath,
I can't express...she is my life...
My soul, my heart, my flesh...

MORRIS: Your wife!!

(Pause.)

So come, dear friend, the hour is nigh:
You now must love...until you die.

From

THE WAR NEXT DOOR
by Tamsin Oglesby

The War Next Door *was first performed at the Tricycle Theatre in February 2007.*

MAX and Sophie find themselves living next door to a wife beater, ALI, and his oppressed wife, Hana, who are middle-eastern immigrants. MAX and Sophie believe they're open-minded but the question of whether they should intervene or not creates an uncomfortable debate between them. However, that's not all. MAX gave ALI some marijuana seeds for his own use and has now discovered that ALI is dealing in drugs, which have been grown from MAX's seeds. MAX is scared that if it's discovered, his career as a barrister will be over, so he tries to discuss the matter. The conversation soon turns ugly.

ALI/MAX

ALI: You know what, Max. I like you and that,
    but what I do in my own house is none of your fucking business,
        mate.

MAX: It is exactly my business.

ALI: I don't even want to have this debate.

MAX: I am a witness – I've actually seen you at it –
    so it's very much my business.

ALI: Yeah? Well whatever you saw, you think you saw,
    it's got fuck all to do with you.

MAX: It has everything to do with me –
    I'm your *neighbour* unfortunately
    so I cannot ignore –
    I will not stand by –
    if I see someone doing something I deplore –

ALI: Fucking – what's your problem, man?
    It's my own business what I do on my own fucking patch.

MAX: Patch?

ALI: Patch, house, whatever, *home*. What's the big deal?

MAX: It's not just *your* business,
    my friend – try saying that to the law
    they might think you're taking the piss.

ALI: You gonna squeal?

MAX: It is *illegal*.

ALI: Go on then. Call the fucking fuzz.

MAX: It is, you know, it is a criminal offence.

ALI: You think they're interested in me? You think they give a fuck
    about my little criminal fence?

MAX: I didn't say I'm going to call them, / I just told you it's not legal.

ALI: Go ahead. Call the cops. Go on. Here's my phone.
    You think you got evidence.

MAX: Look – this isn't about the fucking police
    alright? I just came round to talk. To reason.

In the name of peace.

ALI: That's nice, innit. How polite.

MAX: I'm not interested in the law. I'm a barrister.
That's not what this is about. I'm interested in stopping you before they find out.

ALI: I'm careful.

MAX: No. Careful isn't good enough.
The law is not equivocal when it comes to this sort of stuff.

ALI: But it's not like a frigging drugs ring.
It's not my total income, is it?
It's more a supplement, type thing.

MAX: It is illegal to sell drugs. Full stop.

ALI: Piss in the ocean, mate. Not even a drop.

MAX: How much?

ALI: What?

MAX: How much are you making? From my weed. How much?

ALI: You want a cut?

MAX: No I do not want a cut. I wouldn't touch
it with a barge pole. I want to know how much
you make and who are they – the people who buy it?

ALI: We got a customer base 'bout twenty-five.

MAX: Fuck's sake.

ALI: Thirty tops.

MAX: And who are these – *customer base* – who are these people?

ALI: You want their names?

MAX: No I don't want their fucking names you stupid sod.
I want to know – where do they come from?
How do you know them? How do you know – they're not part of some drug squad?

ALI: What, all of them?

MAX: How do you know you can trust them?

ALI: I don't trust them. Why should I trust them? I don't know them.

MAX: Exactly.

ALI: They just pay me. Cash.
I don't care who they are.
long as they keep coming back
for their hash.

MAX: You should care.

ALI: Don't worry about it, man.
Give yourself a heart attack.

MAX: I am fucking worried about it.

ALI: Well don't fucking worry about it. / I'm not worried about it.

MAX: I am worried about it because, look, okay, listen. I am a
barrister. / And as a barrister – SHUTTUP – as a

ALI: It's only – who cares what I –

MAX: member of the legal profession, I have to be above reproof.
I can't be mixed up with this kind of *trade*.
Now. I haven't done anything wrong
but if a connection can be made –

ALI: You're the supplier innit?

MAX: If a connection can be made between you as the pusher and me
as the person you got them from –

ALI: You gave me the seeds.

MAX: Thank you, yes, wasn't that nice of me? *Gave.*
But the law might not see it as generosity.
The law looks for signs of reciprocity.
Now, you might not care if you get done
but carry on like this and we'll both be in prison
so you've got to fucking stop it.
I gave you that stuff to smoke for your pleasure
not deal on my bloody doorstep for profit.

ALI: My bloody doorstep, not your bloody doorstep.

MAX: Because I am complicit, you see, in your crime,
and if they ever found out – which they will do –
because the way you carry on it's only a matter of time –
I cannot overstate the scale of the disaster that would ensue.
You have no idea –
if they ever found out and traced it back to me.

it would be the complete and total fucking end of my whole entire career.

ALI: Well that's alright then innit, cos I'm not telling them.

MAX: Well that's nice of you, Ali, why don't you give yourself a prize? If you wave it about on the fucking doorstep they don't need telling, do they? They just need eyes.

From

FIVE VISIONS OF THE FAITHFUL
(I am the Knife)
by Torben Betts

Five Visions of the Faithful *was first performed at The White Bear Theatre, London in October 2000.*

Five Visions of the Faithful is a series of short plays which explore the concept and application of cruelty. *I am the Knife* is set within a prison and the INMATE is an enemy of the state who has been sentenced to death. He is visited by the PRIEST who tries to persuade him to sign a confession in order to save his life and be freed. The PRIEST is a very ordinary man with a drinking problem. He sees that the INMATE is everything that he is not: principled, strong and driven. The INMATE is able to endure almost any cruelty to which he is subjected by clinging to his ideals. He will not sign.

PRIEST/INMATE

PRIEST: This is…this is something of an honour for me. (*No answer.*) It would have been nicer, though, to have met you in slightly happier circumstances. (*No answer.*) Are you sure you won't sit? (*No answer.*) You mind if I… (*Pours another drink. Drinks.*)

INMATE: You're an alcoholic?

PRIEST: (*After a pause.*) I am. (*A silence.*) Does that make me slightly more human in your eyes?

INMATE: I never had you down as a god.

PRIEST: No…well…a god I am certainly not. (*A silence.*) I don't think I've ever met anyone as famous as yourself… Makes me a little nervous, actually.

INMATE: Is the smell of my shit upsetting you?

PRIEST: I have to say…

INMATE: I have learned to regard it with equanimity.

PRIEST: I see…

INMATE: It's a part of myself. I will not be disgusted by myself.

PRIEST: Do you mind if I…? (*He reaches for his cigarette packet. He has run out of cigarettes and is forced to relight his previous half-smoked one. He puffs at it desperately.*) Is there nothing you want to say to me?

INMATE: No.

PRIEST: That saddens me.

INMATE: You feel I am missing out?

PRIEST: It often helps to unburden yourself of whatever…

INMATE: Your whole existence has been an appalling waste of time.

PRIEST: (*After a pause.*) Perhaps. (*He drags on the butt.*) You are at peace with the world? You are ready to…?

INMATE: I am.

PRIEST: And you will not sign the…?

INMATE: No!!

PRIEST: You could walk under the sun again. As a free man. You could spend time with your family. Watch your daughter blossom into a woman.

INMATE: I have said my goodbyes.

PRIEST: But your wife…

INMATE: Outwardly she is my loyal supporter, inwardly she aches for compromise.

PRIEST: Surely…

INMATE: Women…they seek proof of our mettle, they spur us on to show ourselves worthy. It is for them that we steal, it is for them that we murder, it is for them that we die.

PRIEST: Well…

INMATE: You have nothing to teach me, you offer no consolation for me.

PRIEST: It is only a signature. Swear to renounce all…

INMATE: Your cowardliness is an affront to my sight.

PRIEST: Yes.

INMATE: Your trembling, your shaking hands…

PRIEST: Yes.

INMATE: I do not have such a long time to live, Father, and so if you'll excuse me, I should like to be alone.

PRIEST: (*After a pause.*) I find it increasingly difficult to abide my own company.

INMATE: That is your cross.

PRIEST: I…I respect your desire for solitude but…you are what I would call a truly honourable man. You are somebody I have always…respected. There are so few people of integrity these days. We…to execute those who… It is an abhorrent waste, is it not?…To snuff out honourable minds. (*No answer.*) I…as I say…it is a great honour to…

INMATE: I am the knife that cuts through your complacency. I am the knife that slits open your over-stuffed belly and makes your self-satisfaction ooze from the wound. I am the knife that causes you pain but only through the pain is there hope of a cure.

(*A silence. The* PRIEST *is in despair. He drinks.*)

PRIEST: I feel so wretched. I do not feel worthy of…

INMATE: Then go.

PRIEST: I think I must…

INMATE: Go and drink your vapid days away, dishing out your uncertain crumbs of comfort to the bewildered flock.

PRIEST: We must all survive. Somehow. Those born without talent must…

INMATE: Go.

PRIEST: If you would only sign…

INMATE: Get out.

(*The* PRIEST *stands weakly. He slowly approaches the* INMATE.)

PRIEST: I'm sorry to have wasted your time… If I might have the honour of shaking your hand…

INMATE: Your breath reeks.

PRIEST: I apologise.

INMATE: Good luck to you.

(*They shake hands. A long silence as they stare at each other. The* PRIEST *seems to be holding onto the* INMATE *for dear life. They finally disengage, the* PRIEST *still staring deeply into the other man's eyes.*)

PRIEST: (*Suddenly, despairingly.*) But the beatings…! How do you take the beatings? Sleeping on the floor there? With only a bucket? Waiting for your death. How…how can you stand it?

(*A silence.*)

INMATE: Withstanding violence is the prisoner's daily grind. It is not so different on the streets, however. In the offices. They are at least fair here. I can count the punches. It's the honest face of clockwatching.

PRIEST: Surely you owe it to the people to stay alive? What you stand for must not simply be exterminated with you! Surely a small reconciliation…

INMATE: There is nothing more contemptible than the spectacle of the philosophy unadhered to.

From

THE POSSIBILITIES
(Reasons for the Fall of Emperors)
by Howard Barker

The Possibilities *was first performed in 1988 at the
Almeida Theatre in London.*

A collection of ten short plays explore some disturbing moral
dilemmas and ambiguities in different times and cultures. In
Reasons for the Fall of Emperors we find Emperor ALEXANDER
in his tent at the end of a terrible day on the battlefield. He is
tired of fighting (and a little weepy with it) and strikes up a
conversation with a GROOM who is there to clean his boots.

ALEXANDER/GROOM

ALEXANDER: Come in, who's there!

(*Pause. A peasant enters, holding the EMPEROR's boots.*)

GROOM: Excellency?

ALEXANDER: Who are you?

GROOM: I am a groom. I am polishing the Emperor's boots. If the sound of the brushes offends him I will go behind the horse lines, perhaps he will not hear it there, but you can't be sure.

ALEXANDER: You are a peasant?

GROOM: I am. Doing six years' service with the regiment.

ALEXANDER: How does a peasant sleep?

GROOM: He sleeps better than the Emperor.

ALEXANDER: Why, do the sounds of his brothers dying not disturb his rest?

GROOM: They were born in pain. They slit the throats of oxen. They beat and sometimes kill their wives. They die of famine in filthy huts and fall into machinery. The Turk is swift with the knife, though not as swift as the Bulgarian. As for the cry, it's brief. The ox protests as well. Who hears him?

ALEXANDER: I think of this. I think of the grief in distant villages, the orphans who scour the long white lane…

GROOM: They say the Emperor is a sensitive man. Some say they've seen him weep in hospitals.

ALEXANDER: He does.

GROOM: But the war must go on, at least until it stops.

ALEXANDER: (*Pause.*) When I hear you, little brother, I know I must build more schools. Do you read?

GROOM: Read what?

ALEXANDER: The Bible.

GROOM: No, but I listen, and agree with every word of it.

ALEXANDER: Is it not often contradictory?

GROOM: I agree with all the contradictions, too. As for schools, if I could read the gentlemen's books, I should only lose sleep, and then the battle would certainly be lost and the Turks would slit not only our throats but the Emperor's too, and that would surely be the end of the world.

ALEXANDER: Do you love the Emperor?

GROOM: It is impossible not to love him!

ALEXANDER: But he weeps so much!

GROOM: I forgive him for that. I had an aunt who wept continually but could not say why. She just wept.

ALEXANDER: He weeps for you…

GROOM: And we for him! We do! Shall I get on with the boots? He will need them in the morning.

(*He goes to pick them up.*)

ALEXANDER: I THINK THAT'S WRONG.

GROOM: (*Stopping.*) I apologise to His Excellency. I am a boot polisher and unable to follow arguments –

ALEXANDER: LIAR.

GROOM: I am sure we all lie but only by accident –

ALEXANDER: YOU ARE NOT SO WOODEN AS –

GROOM: No, obviously not –

ALEXANDER: AS YOU PRETEND.

(*Pause. They stare at one another.*)

Oh, little brother, I could kiss you on the mouth…

GROOM: My mouth, as all my flesh, is at Your Excellency's service…

(*The EMPEROR sits on the bed and weeps silently. The GROOM watches. Pause.*)

My brother died today. So when I get home I shall have twice as many children. Life…! He was a good father and drank so much he punched their eyes black, one after another! Still, they'll weep! And if I die…!

ALEXANDER: Don't go on…

GROOM: There's a murderer in all of us, God says so, so a couple will be hanged and a couple flogged, and a stranger hacked to pieces in his drawing room, but then the war has little wars inside it like one of His Excellency's decorated eggs –

ALEXANDER: I SAID I –

GROOM: I only meant – it is not good for an emperor to weep in front of a peasant.

ALEXANDER: On the contrary, what is your love worth if it attaches itself only to a dummy? THAT SOUND!

GROOM: It is a good sound, believe me! It is the sound of sacrifice, you should hear it as another hymn to your house, different in tone but not in quality, from the crowd's gasp at your coronation. The Emperor should know the people will go on dying until the villages are dry sticks and the cattle skeletons. The dead only encourage further sacrifice. Along a road of skulls he might dance if he chose to…!

ALEXANDER: (*Pause.*) I will put an end to slavery. I will abolish feudalism. I will place teachers in every hamlet. I will break from stooping habit and the ingrained servility of serfs. I will run electricity to every hut and create a corps of critics who will yell at every inhumanity!

GROOM: (*Pause.*) I must finish the boots. It will be dawn and they need all hands at the batteries.

ALEXANDER: Undress me.

(*Pause. The GROOM puts down the boots. He goes to the EMPEROR and unbuttons his tunic. He removes it.*)

Your fingers do not tremble…

GROOM: Why should they? If they trembled it could only be because I was disloyal or entertained some thought of treason, or even that I felt my position shameful in some way, which I do not. How much clothing should I remove?

ALEXANDER: The Emperor will be naked?

GROOM: He will be cold.

(*A cry in the distance.*)

ALEXANDER: Then it will be him who trembles.

(*The GROOM proceeds.*)

Oh, there is shit in my pants!

GROOM: Yes. Has His Excellency a chill on the bowel?

ALEXANDER: He was seized by terror during the attack…

GROOM: It was a terrible battle. Our soldiers climbed each other to the Turkish trench.

ALEXANDER: I wept, and I shat…

GROOM: (*Folding the clothes.*) The error was the lack of high explosive shell. The trenches were undamaged.

ALEXANDER: And I pleaded, blow the retreat!

GROOM: Yes, I heard the bugle! Which was I think unfortunate, because the retreating men collided with the second wave and more died in the confusion than if the attack had been pressed –

ALEXANDER: That was me – and only me –

GROOM: It is the Emperor's right to have bugles blown at his whim –

ALEXANDER: They died, and yet more died…

GROOM: Better luck tomorrow. Shall you keep your socks on? The earth is damp.

ALEXANDER: NO SOCKS.

GROOM: The Emperor is goose-fleshed, shall I massage his limb?

ALEXANDER: NO MASSAGE.

(*He stands naked, shivering. A distant cry.*)

You are dressed and I am naked. You are strong and I am weak. You are fine and I am stunted.

GROOM: Yes.

ALEXANDER: Justify your failure to assassinate me, then.

GROOM: Justify…?

ALEXANDER: Yes, justify it.

GROOM: The Emperor takes me for a wolf. I am offended he should think I am a wolf. But let him offend where he wishes. He is the Emperor.

(*A pause. ALEXANDER looks into him. Suddenly he shouts.*)

ALEXANDER: FLOG THIS MAN! HEY! FLOG THIS MAN!

(*The OFFICER enters.*)

GROOM: What for…?

ALEXANDER: FLOG AND FLOG THIS MAN!

GROOM: In Jesus' name, what for…?

(*The OFFICER takes the man by the shoulder.*)

ALEXANDER: What for? No reason. Flog him for no reason.

From

PROVING MR JENNINGS
by James Walker

Proving Mr Jennings *was first produced at the*
Courtyard Theatre, London in 2004.

Proving Mr Jennings is a tragi-comic cautionary tale which
explores what could happen when government hysteria
about terrorism is out of control. CHARLES JENNINGS QC has
(supposedly) just had a heart transplant. However, he wakes
up from the anaesthetic, strapped to the bed in what appears
to be a bunker. His doctor, MR GIBBONS, has some bad news:
when his chest was opened up they found a ticking time bomb
there instead of a heart. And so MR JENNINGS is accused of
being a suicide bomber. He tries to defend himself, despite
being tortured and held against his will. Unfortunately, his wife
believes the government and has left him for GIBBONS (which is
why, in the scene below, GIBBONS is so shaken when he thinks
she is dead).

GIBBONS/JENNINGS

GIBBONS: Mr Jennings, there's something I need to discuss with you –

JENNINGS: For the first time since my youth, I feel truly alive!

GIBBONS: Yes, of course – however –

JENNINGS: (*Oblivious in his rapture.*) Oh I know that for reasons of legality you can't divulge the identity of the person whose… (*Correcting himself.*) – sorry, saint – whose heart I carry within me thanks to you – thanks to you both. Oh, the wonders of modern science! You! You, Doctor, with your teams of dedicated back-up staff and nurses – who aren't back-up at all! No – they've got the right to be appreciated for the angels they are! You all, collectively, you the National Health Service are responsible for the miracle that I carry inside me. NOW!

GIBBONS: Mr Jennings, we're rather pressed for time –

JENNINGS: I take back what I said earlier about the Health Service – I take it back whole-heartedly… (*Tickled at his own joke.*) Whole-heartedly!

GIBBONS: I'm not sure you realise just how precarious your present situation is.

JENNINGS: Oh, I realise well enough! For the first time in my life I know what it feels like to be on the brink of something!

GIBBONS: Actually, that's what I wanted to talk to you about –

JENNINGS: (*Deaf.*) Do you have a charity of preference, Doctor?

GIBBONS: (*Cutting in.*) Would you please listen to me for a –

JENNINGS: (*Interrupting the interruption.*) I know it's hard for a man of the professions to accept handouts. Let's just say the next time you find yourself in legal hot water, not that you would – not a man of your stamp –

GIBBONS: There's something rather pressing I think you should know.

(*Something is wrong.*)

JENNINGS: (*Shrewdly.*) You put a black man's heart in? (*Undismayed.*) Splendid! Life's too short for unwarranted prejudice.

GIBBONS: No. It's nothing like that.

JENNINGS: (*A trifle deflated.*) Oh.

GIBBONS: You see, when we opened you up we found there was nothing there.

JENNINGS: No matter, no matter. The most important thing is that it's done, that's what it boils down to – the result – (*Dawning.*) I'm sorry…what did you say?

GIBBONS: First of all, let me make it clear that I've never been one to shirk responsibility. But some things are simply unavoidable. You see, from the X-ray we saw clearly that what we assumed to be the heart was situated on the left side of the thorax, but in actual fact…what we were seeing on the X-ray turned out to be not on the left at all.

JENNINGS: (*Confused.*) The heart?

GIBBONS: …Yes.

JENNINGS: Not on the left?

GIBBONS: No.

JENNINGS: It was on the wrong side?

GIBBONS: We call it dextrocardia. It's a congenital condition. Extremely rare.

JENNINGS: You didn't know this *before* you opened me up?

GIBBONS: As I say, it's extremely rare –

JENNINGS: You did do an X-ray?

GIBBONS: Of course.

JENNINGS: Wouldn't that make it fairly clear? I thought that was what an X-ray was for.

GIBBONS: I don't want to bore you with technicalities. Suffice to say it was nobody's fault. A straightforward example of Photo-Phobic-Inverted-Orienteering-Perception-Disorder on the part of the radiologist.

(*Pause.*)

JENNINGS: You looked at the X-ray the wrong way round.

GIBBONS: Not personally.

JENNINGS: (*Generously.*) Well, there's no use crying over split ribs. You got there in the end. Now the operation's done I wouldn't care if you told me I'd had a stone in there!

GIBBONS: Mr Jennings I have some bad news for you.

(*Pause.*)

JENNINGS: (*Playful.*) It was a stone?

GIBBONS: No, it wasn't a stone.

JENNINGS: (*Suddenly serious, anticipating the worst.*) My wife's dead…

GIBBONS: (*Stopped in his tracks.*) She is?

JENNINGS: (*Confused.*) I don't know…

GIBBONS: (*Deeply alarmed.*) She's your wife, for Pete's sake!

JENNINGS: I thought that's what you were going to tell me –

GIBBONS: That she's your wife?

JENNINGS: That she's died in some horrible car crash –

GIBBONS: (*Genuinely shaken.*) Oh my God…

JENNINGS: I don't know if she has –

GIBBONS: But you think she might?

JENNINGS: I don't know!

GIBBONS: When did you hear?

JENNINGS: Just now –

GIBBONS: Who told you?

JENNINGS: You did!

GIBBONS: That she's dead?

JENNINGS: (*His worst fears confirmed.*) DEAD!

GIBBONS: I never said that!

JENNINGS: That's not what you were going to tell me?

GIBBONS: No!

JENNINGS: Thank God!

GIBBONS: So she's alright?

JENNINGS: I think so –

GIBBONS: What a relief! (*With genuine feeling.*) That could have been very tragic indeed.

(*Pause.*)

JENNINGS: You're sweating, Doctor. Are you sure you're well?

GIBBONS: (*Ploughing on.*) I'm fine… (*Looking at his watch.*) Look, Mr Jennings, I came to tell you something quite specific and we're running out of time –

JENNINGS: Relax, Doctor. Don't run yourself into the ground. Thanks to you the years stretch out before me!

GIBBONS: Mr Jennings, I want you to realise that this is as hard for me as it is for you, but…during the course of the operation, after we opened up the right side of the thorax after an initial blunder which – as I say – was not entirely our own –

JENNINGS: (*Chivvying.*) Yes, yes…

GIBBONS: Of course…well…it happened that once we exposed your right side, which is where the X-rays had initially indicated your heart would be… (*Pause.*) …I don't know quite how to put this… but we…well…

JENNINGS: Yes?

GIBBONS: Didn't find a heart at all.

(*JENNINGS tries to rationalise this news.*)

JENNINGS: You definitely looked?

GIBBONS: Oh yes.

JENNINGS: (*Helpfully.*) It wasn't tucked away somewhere? Behind a lung, perhaps?

(*GIBBONS looks seriously at him.*)

You must have found something. I was alive, wasn't I?

GIBBONS: In a manner of speaking.

JENNINGS: Well? There must have been something!

GIBBONS: Yes.

JENNINGS: Spit it out! Whatever it is, it can't be that bad…

GIBBONS: (*Directly.*) We found a bomb.

JENNINGS: …I'm still here!

(*Pause.*)

(*Hardly audible.*) A what?

GIBBONS: I'm so sorry.

(*Pause.*)

JENNINGS: Could you repeat that?

GIBBONS: Of course. (*Repeating exactly.*) We found a bomb.

JENNINGS: A…bomb?

GIBBONS: Yes.

JENNINGS: As in…(*Gestures an explosion.*)

(*GIBBONS nods solemnly.*

A beat.

JENNINGS bursts out laughing.)

Oh priceless! Oh I like that! Very funny indeed…you chaps are a hoot!

(*JENNINGS laughs uproariously.*

GIBBONS is not smiling.)

Well go on, Doctor! Don't be such an old toad! I think it's brilliant! (*Imitating.*) 'You have a bomb instead of a heart, Mr Jennings.' I bet you tell all your patients that!

(*He laughs again.*)

GIBBONS: I wish I had better news.

(*JENNINGS' laughter gutters out.*)

I really don't know what else to say.

JENNINGS: You're serious.

GIBBONS: I'm afraid I am.

(*Pause.*)

JENNINGS: (*Tapping his chest in disbelief.*) In here?

GIBBONS: I wouldn't have believed it myself –

JENNINGS: You're pulling my leg!

GIBBONS: That's what the disposal squad told me.

JENNINGS: *Disposal squad!*

From

THE LAST CONFESSION
by Roger Crane

The Last Confession *was first performed in April 2007 at The Chichester Festival Theatre. It was subsequently toured and produced in the West End by Duncan C Weldon and Paul Elliott for Triumph Entertainment Ltd and Theatre Royal Haymarket Productions.*

In 1978 a little-known Cardinal from Venice was elected to succeed Pope Paul VI. A compromise candidate, he took the name Pope John Paul I, and quickly showed himself to be liberal in his ideas, which was not to everyone's taste. Thirty-three days later he was dead. *The Last Confession* provides a hypothetical explanation as to what happened through the final confession of CARDINAL GIOVANNI BENELLI (formerly an Archbishop and latterly, at the time of his confession, Cardinal of Florence). BENELLI was instrumental in helping Pope John Paul to power and conducts an investigation into his death, alongside of Cardinal Ottaviani and Cardinal Felici, two conservative cardinals. In this scene BENELLI is questioning CARDINAL JEAN VILLOT, The Secretary of State of the Vatican, who was a sworn enemy to the Pope.

VILLOT/BENELLI

VILLOT: (*To BENELLI.*) Try to be brief.

BENELLI: We are here to discuss the death of a Pope.

VILLOT: All men die, even Popes.

BENELLI: It is one thing to die; it is another thing to be killed.

VILLOT: No one killed the Pope.

BENELLI: Tell me about Pope Paul.

VILLOT: What?

BENELLI: What did you think of him?

(*VILLOT looks briefly at OTTAVIANI and FELICI.*)

VILLOT: He was a great Pope. He was trained in the discipline of the Curia. He was learned, a scholar, an intellectual, a man who cared deeply for the Church and who thought carefully before coming to decisions.

BENELLI: What was his greatest achievement?

VILLOT: His encyclical on birth control.

BENELLI: What do you want in the next Pope?

VILLOT: A greater Paul. A man to carry his work forward, a man of authority and discipline.

BENELLI: And compassion?

VILLOT: Compassion is for priests, not for Popes.

BENELLI: And not for Secretaries of State.

VILLOT: My function is to run the Church.

BENELLI: Yet you let Luciani change the investiture ceremony.

VILLOT: It was a ceremony a thousand years old. He changed it on a whim, as if it were just the organisation of a garden party.

BENELLI: And you let him.

VILLOT: He was the Pope.

BENELLI: And as long as he was the Pope you had to obey.

VILLOT: Yes.

BENELLI: Tell us about John Paul's feelings toward Paul's encyclical on birth control.

VILLOT: (*Pause.*) We would have convinced him.

BENELLI: Of what?

VILLOT: That Pope Paul was right.

BENELLI: How could you if you were no longer here?

VILLOT: What do you mean?

BENELLI: You were leaving Rome.

VILLOT: I had no intention of leaving Rome.

BENELLI: On September the twenty-eighth, the day the Pope died, he told you that he was removing you as Secretary of State.

VILLOT: How dare you say that?

BENELLI: I don't say it, Cardinal Suenens does.

You came to see the Pope one final time.

VILLOT: I saw the Pope frequently.

BENELLI: You had just been removed. You returned to try to get the Pope to change his mind.

VILLOT: He was going to destroy everything that Pope Paul accomplished.

BENELLI: And you failed.

VILLOT: He wouldn't listen.

BENELLI: And the papers were already drawn up. The papers removing you and others.

VILLOT: He had papers.

BENELLI: And that night he took them to bed with him.

VILLOT: He was going to remove the best people in the Curia.

BENELLI: He was the Pope and you had to obey.

VILLOT: I did not have to obey.

BENELLI: As long as he lived you had to obey. (*Pause.*) What happened that evening of September the twenty-eighth? Was it the coffee? Was it the sweets he loved? Was it his bottle of pills?

VILLOT: There is no evidence he was poisoned.

BENELLI: You destroyed the evidence.

VILLOT: No Pope is more important than the Church. The Curia has defeated greater Popes than John Paul.

BENELLI: And how would you have stopped him?

VILLOT: I buried him in paper.

BENELLI: But he made decisions.

VILLOT: And we told him no.

BENELLI: Again and again you told him no.

VILLOT: Yes.

BENELLI: And day after day the piles of paper grew higher.

VILLOT: Yes.

BENELLI: For a year nothing had been decided. Now in one month you poured on his shoulders every problem you could find.

VILLOT: He was the Pope. He had to make the decisions.

BENELLI: And when he made them, you told him no.

VILLOT: He was wrong. (*BENELLI stares at him.*) I am the Secretary of State. It is my right to tell the Pope he is wrong.

BENELLI: It is the Pope's right to make the final decisions.

VILLOT: Error has no rights.

BENELLI: Are you saying the Pope was in error?

VILLOT: Every word. Every action.

BENELLI: Who are you to judge the Pope?

VILLOT: He wasn't a Pope. He was a country priest that you pushed into the papacy. He was your Pope, not ours.

BENELLI: And this country priest had ideas of his own. Ideas he was willing to fight for.

VILLOT: He would have destroyed the Church.

BENELLI: Who made you the final arbiter?

VILLOT: The Curia is the Church.

BENELLI: He would have changed the Curia.

VILLOT: I would have stopped him.

BENELLI: He removed you. There was only one way you could stop him.

VILLOT: I did not murder the Pope.

BENELLI: You drove him. You couldn't change him. So you isolated him and drove him.

VILLOT: (*Stands up.*) Yes, I drove him. I drove him day and night.

BENELLI: He was in error. He was wrong.

VILLOT: He was the error.

BENELLI: He would have destroyed the Church.

VILLOT: Yes.

BENELLI: He had to die.

VILLOT: Yes.

BENELLI: He had to die for the Church.

VILLOT: Yes, I drove him – I worked him – I drove him until his body – until he died. Yes… God help me…I killed the Pope. (*The room is silent.*)

BENELLI: (*Softly.*) We all killed him.

PART THREE
FEMALE/MALE
DUOLOGUES

From

VIRGINS
by John Retallack

Virgins *was first performed at the Junction Theatre,
Cambridge, in July 2006. It is published in* Company of
Angels, *which includes three other plays by John Retallack:*
Hannah and Hanna, Club Asylum *and* Risk.

Virgins is described as a 'family drama about sexual politics',
which explores some of the issues surrounding teenage sexual
experimentation. Seventeen year old JACK went to a party
where he took drugs and had (unprotected) sex for the first
time with SADIE, whom he really liked. Unfortunately he can't
remember much about it at all. His friend, Ben, told him that
he later had sex with another girl at the same party, which he
can't recall. A few days later he discovered that he'd caught a
painful sexually transmitted infection. He calls SADIE after a
visit to the clinic.

SADIE/JACK

SADIE: (*On phone.*) Hullo…?

JACK: Hullo is that Sadie?

SADIE: Yes, it's me, hullo Jack, I'd given up –

JACK: Sadie, I'm sorry, I was going to call you but I lost your mobile number –

SADIE: It's alright, how you doing?

JACK: I'm alright, how you doing?

SADIE: I'm alright… You?

SADIE: Yeah I'm good

JACK: You know we were together?

SADIE: At Carol Smith's?

JACK: Yeah, at the party

SADIE: Yeah…

JACK: Something I should tell you

SADIE: What?

JACK: You know we had sex?

SADIE: Yes Jack, what?

JACK: I've had one or two problems – down below – and…well…I've got an STI

SADIE: What's that?

JACK: A sexually transmitted infection

SADIE: Oh

JACK: I checked it out and now I've got some treatment –

SADIE: Is this some kind of horrible joke you're playing?

JACK: No Sadie not at all, I've just come out of the clinic and the first thing that they tell you must do is to phone your partner

SADIE: You're not my partner

JACK: I know I'm not but I was then wasn't I? At the time?

SADIE: Why didn't you tell me?

JACK: I'm telling you now aren't I?

SADIE: I thought you had a condom

JACK: I did have a condom

SADIE: Didn't you use it?

JACK: No

SADIE: Why?

JACK: I forgot

SADIE: I don't *believe* this

JACK: I'm really sorry Sadie

SADIE: This is awful

JACK: I can't remember everything properly –

SADIE: Already?

JACK: But I'm right we did, didn't we?

SADIE: Did what?

JACK: Have sex? Together?

SADIE: Yes

JACK: Right. Just want to be sure.

SADIE: What am I supposed to do?

JACK: You should go to the clinic at the hospital. It's no big deal. It's round the back. They just give you a pill. It's simple.

SADIE: I haven't got anything

JACK: It doesn't always show – in women

SADIE: Are you saying you got this disease from me?

JACK: Not exactly – according to Ben I could have got it from you or someone else

SADIE: Who?

JACK: I'm not saying Sadie because I don't know if it's true

SADIE: Ben? Ben Mathews?

JACK: Yeah, Ben…

SADIE: So what did he say?

JACK: Ben says that after we were together, I got totally off my face –

SADIE: What do you mean you could have caught it from someone else?

JACK: According to Ben – after you left the party –

SADIE: I didn't leave – *you* vanished! I looked for you everywhere and I left feeling a slag, just a fuck in the dark and not a word from you since – till this!

'Oh hello Sadie – sorry – you've got AIDS.'

JACK: It's not AIDS! The clinic say it's an infection, you'll be alright if you just go to the clinic

SADIE: Oh shut up about the clinic! What does Ben say happened after I left – who were you with?

JACK: Beth. Beth Green

SADIE: *Beth Green*!? Jack!

JACK: Yup – That's what Ben says. I don't remember a thing about it; I never ever spoke to Beth Green. Ben says that I also –

SADIE: I don't want to know Jack!

JACK: You asked me!

SADIE: Don't call me again!

JACK: Well now you know. I'm really sorry Sadie, I didn't want to upset you but now you know.

SADIE: And why do you think *I* gave it to *you*? – it sounds more like *you* gave it to *me* – and half the other girls who were at the party!

JACK: Aren't you exaggerating?

SADIE: You don't know what you're doing, do you Jack? You're not even responsible for your own actions – you don't even know where you put it, you idiot!

JACK: Look Sadie –

SADIE: I hope you caught it from Beth Green!

JACK: Listen…

SADIE: I hope you die!

JACK: Sadie!

SADIE: Oh fuck off Jack!

From

DEADEYE

by Amber Lone

Deadeye *was first performed at The Door,*
Birmingham Repertory Theatre in October 2006.

Deadeye explores the reality of inner city life for second
generation Asians, who are caught between two worlds. TARIQ
and DEEMA are brother and sister, living in Birmingham. DEEMA
is trying to do the right thing – going to college, working
part-time and supporting her parents (who are having financial
troubles). However, TARIQ is messed up with drugs and living on
the streets. His successful cousin, Jimmy, who usually supplies
him, is missing some money and thinks TARIQ has taken it.
Jimmy meets with DEEMA and threatens to beat up TARIQ when
he finds him. A few days later DEEMA finds TARIQ on the street
and tries to warn him.

DEEMA/TARIQ

DEEMA: Oi.

(*TARIQ jumps.*)

TARIQ: For fuck's sake…what are you doin' here?

DEEMA: I was passin'.

TARIQ: You flippin' followin' me?

DEEMA: Said I was passin' and I needed to talk to you.

TARIQ: You're going on like some sort of nutter Deem. I'm alright.

DEEMA: No you're not.

TARIQ: We'll talk about it later right.

(*TARIQ stops to lean against a wall.*)

DEEMA: We can't talk about it later.

TARIQ: Please man…my legs are killin' me.

DEEMA: Mom and dad…we've got some trouble at home.

TARIQ: Aaah! Fuck.

DEEMA: What is wrong with you?

TARIQ: Legs are hurting…like someone's driven over 'em with a truck.

(*DEEMA leans next to him and starts to roll a cigarette.*)

Can I have one?

(*DEEMA passes him the rolled-up cigarette. TARIQ takes a drag and bends over then tries to stretch, all the time acting as if he's dying. DEEMA is motionless.*)

DEEMA: It's your own doing.

TARIQ: Need your help…I'm desperate.

DEEMA: You're always desperate. Meanwhile I go to college, apply for jobs, get the shopping Mum needs, help pay the bills, wash the dishes, make the roti…tell Dad lies about where you are…

TARIQ: Didn't ask you to. Did I ask you?

DEEMA: There's enough to think about.

TARIQ: It ain't that bad.

DEEMA: Yes it is.

TARIQ: Stop makin' a big deal of everything man. In time…

DEEMA: We've got no time. The house is being repossessed.

TARIQ: Just scare tactics.

DEEMA: How is Dad gonna get the money?

TARIQ: Bastard…

DEEMA: What…?

(*TARIQ is hitting his head with his hands.*)

TARIQ: I can't walk…feels like I'm dying…if I don't…if I don't get it…I…I'm gonna end up doin' something stupid…can't even sit down. Some dog tried to bite my arse.

DEEMA: See I don't think I can take any more of all this shit…I just can't deal with it.

TARIQ: You should've seen it. Fucken great mangy thing…down by the railway bridge… Was just walken' past this 'ouse…I mean the front door…it was open and nobody was around… People round 'ere take silly chances man… I walk up to it…tryin' to be a good neighbour…and this woman sets her Alsatian on me. He's going for me like he ain't eaten for days and she's flapping her arms up and down screamin' thieves like me should go back to their own country… I'm goin': I was born 'ere bitch… The cheek of it Deem…she's the one who should have been locked up… I mean I could get rabies…I should get rabies…then I'd sue her arse.

DEEMA: Shut up Tariq…I've had it with ya…try my hardest and I mess it up. All this trouble. I had an interview…cabin crew…I could've bin seeing Rome, Paris…bloody Marrakech.

TARIQ: What interview?

DEEMA: It don't matter.

(*DEEMA sits on the ground and TARIQ calms down, slowly making his way down to her clutching his leg as he does.*)

TARIQ: C'mon sis…that's wicked. You know Dad…last minute something'll turn up. You'll see…and you've got a job…that's good…you've gotta think about yerself. That's what I'm gonna do.

DEEMA: I haven't got a job.

TARIQ: You just said man.

DEEMA: I had an interview Tariq.

TARIQ: You'll get it no probs.

DEEMA: I cancelled okay. Said I couldn't go.

(*Beat.*)

TARIQ: What you do that for?

DEEMA: Jimmy came round for ya.

TARIQ: Fuck him.

DEEMA: He threatened me Tariq…

TARIQ: What's the arsehole said… I'll –

DEEMA: Said he wants the money you took.

TARIQ: What you talking about?

DEEMA: I'm speaking a foreign language ain't I? You can't get out of this one. He's angry. Said he's gonna sort you out. In Mum's house Tariq… You're gonna drag them into it…what the fuck are you doing?

TARIQ: I'm fixing things Deem.

DEEMA: He isn't gonna go away. Dunno what he could do.

TARIQ: All mouth man. Jimmy ain't even bin inside. He's a wannabe.

DEEMA: They don't need this… We've got other shit to do. I've got other shit to do Tariq… Just get him his money… You have still got it ain't ya?

TARIQ: I haven't got his fuckin' money man.

DEEMA: How long you gonna hide for?

TARIQ: Listen to me. I'm gonna give this up…I'm gonna detox. I've gotta be there with ya…start working… Fed up with all this…you don't know how fed up I am. I went to the clinic.

DEEMA: You did.

TARIQ: Told ya…I ain't messin' about.

DEEMA: Just come see Mum and Dad right. Maybe we can deal with it together.

TARIQ: It's all gonna change. Don't want to be like this any more.

DEEMA: That's good Taz.

TARIQ: I've been cutting down… By next week, I'll be almost clean…but it's fuckin' hurtin' sis. I need a bit of money…just to get enough to cover the pain.

(*DEEMA stands up chucking her cigarette away.*)

DEEMA: Have to go.

TARIQ: So can you help us?

DEEMA: With what Tariq?

TARIQ: You heard what I said man…

DEEMA: Ain't got nothing.

TARIQ: Your wages.

DEEMA: My wages.

TARIQ: Twenny quid that's all.

DEEMA: We have to get the phone reconnected.

(*TARIQ pulls out his giro book, stuffed in the back of his jeans pocket and hands it to her. Beat.*)

TARIQ: It's due a week today. / You collect it and take your cut.

DEEMA: Next week.

TARIQ: Please. (*Beat.*) You watch…it's all gonna change. Stop worrying and do your work. You can't keep takin' everythin' to heart. We know what we're doing.

DEEMA: You'll come home? See if we can sort this out?

TARIQ: Told you…I'll see Mum, talk to Dad…say hello an' that.

(*Beat.*)

DEEMA: Yeah?

TARIQ: Yeah.

(*DEEMA takes his hand and he pulls away.*)

I'm not a kid man. (*Beat.*) Can I still 'ave that score then?

(*Lights fade.*)

From

EVERY BREATH
by Judith Johnson

Every Breath *was first toured to London Schools between March and April 2006.*

Every Breath debates the controversial issue of animal use in biomedical research. ANITA, is a twenty-one year old science graduate who is about to embark on a PhD exploring the way genes work in the hearts and livers of mice. This brings her into direct conflict with her eighteen year old brother SONNY, who has become increasingly concerned about animal testing. In fact he has begun to protest at the new laboratory where ANITA will be conducting her research. SONNY is asthmatic and decides that he doesn't want to take any medication that has been researched or tested on animals. Unfortunately his life is at risk without medication and he has been hospitalised after a severe attack. ANITA visits the hospital to try and persuade him to reconsider by presenting him with all the facts. She hovers in the doorway of SONNY's hospital room, where he's reading a magazine.

ANITA/SONNY

ANITA: Not speaking to me little bro?

SONNY: (*Irritated.*) Don't be silly.

> (*ANITA comes in and sits next to the bed. SONNY continues to read the mag.*)

ANITA: I've, er, got some information for you. About asthma medicines.

SONNY: (*Still reading.*) What d'you mean, information?

ANITA: A friend of mine, a scientist, he does exactly the kind of asthma testing you're worried about. I thought it might help you to know what really goes on. Then you can make a clear decision about your medication.

SONNY: I've already made a clear decision.

ANITA: (*Getting up.*) Right. I'll go then.

SONNY: (*Looking up.*) He'll make it sound like nothing.

ANITA: I'm just trying to help Sonny.

> (*Beat.*)

SONNY: (*Begrudging.*) Go on then.

ANITA: Sure?

SONNY: Go on. Before I change my mind.

ANITA: Okay. (*Sits back down.*) The mice used are genetically modified okay? They're created specially for testing asthma medicines.

SONNY: That doesn't make it okay Anita. Scientists playing God again.

ANITA: It means that they're exactly right for the tests, they get the most accurate results.

SONNY: They just see them as tools, not living breathing animals. Are you saying they deliberately create asthma-suffering mice?

ANITA: Yes.

SONNY: Oh great.

ANITA: (*Sighs.*) Am I going to get through this email or are you going to have a nervous breakdown on every single point?

SONNY: Go on.

ANITA: Okay. (*Reading.*) 'For asthma research we use the mouse's inhalation routes, which can be the whole body, or the nose only. Whole body is done in a special chamber. Nose only requires the animals to be restrained with plastic tubes.'

SONNY: So. They basically force them to inhale asthma drugs to see if it harms them?

ANITA: To see what the effects are, not just if it harms them. And force isn't the right word.

SONNY: Excuse me, 'restrained with plastic tubes'? They tie them down, they make them asthmatic so they can't breathe, so they feel just like I did, like I had a slab of concrete on my chest, choking me to death. Then they make them inhale something that may not even make them feel better!

ANITA: (*Shrugs.*) I don't think it's that bad.

SONNY: Not that bad! How would you like it? Why can't they find *another* way to test stuff?

ANITA: There isn't another way. Maybe in the future... [something will be developed]

SONNY: Not in my future.

ANITA: You might not have a future if you don't take the medication!

SONNY: How can I take it after what you've just told me?

ANITA: Look, Sonny, you just have to face it! You have no alternative. Yes, animals have suffered and died...

SONNY: (*Cutting in.*) They're still suffering and dying!

ANITA: Yes. But as little as possible and thousands of human lives are saved!! 1400 people in Britain still die from asthma every year. Imagine how big that would be if the work with animals hadn't been done.

SONNY: How many animals have died? I bet it's a lot more than 1400.

ANITA: I don't know! I don't care!

SONNY: You really don't care that animals are hurt, and sometimes hurt really badly?

ANITA: I care a bit but I care more about the people who benefit from it!

SONNY: That's like me saying it's alright for me to steal someone's money because I benefit from it.

ANITA: It's not!

SONNY: It is Anita! There must be other ways.

ANITA: Oh I give up!

(*She gets up*.)

You are so selfish.

SONNY: I'm selfish. What are you? You don't even think about animals, you're too busy thinking about your precious work.

ANITA: Will you change the record.

SONNY: You change the record. You haven't even tried to see it from my point of view.

ANITA: What?

SONNY: You just assume that because you're cleverer than me, because you've taken loads of exams and read millions of books, then you're right. Mice are warm, living, breathing animals. What right have you got to hurt them?

ANITA: Alright…don't take your medication then. Don't bloody take it. Risk your life! Be a martyr for your…stupid cause. I wanted to help you but you've never accepted help from me. You just throw it back in my face every time. I don't know what I've done to make you hate me so much!!

(*ANITA leaves. She is near to tears.*)

SONNY: (*Amazed.*) Anita!

From

TENDER
by Abi Morgan

Tender *was first produced by Birmingham Repertory Theatre
Company with Hampstead Theatre and Theatre Royal,
Plymouth, at Hampstead Theatre in September 2001.*

Tender is all about searching for connections and relationships
in a big city. TASH is in her late twenties/early thirties and hasn't
settled down: she changes jobs and lovers regularly. SQUEAL is
a hospital doctor in his late twenties/early thirties as well. In
this scene they try to cope with the morning after of a one
night stand (although nothing really happened). It's set in
TASH's London flat and SQUEAL is dressed in TASH's dressing
gown and is peering into the fridge. TASH enters in a towel and
shower cap.

TASH/SQUEAL

TASH: Back. Second shelf.

SQUEAL: (*Sniffing carton.*) It's off.

TASH: I'm making cheese.

SQUEAL: It doesn't matter.

TASH: It was a joke. (*Beat.*) I don't eat breakfast…

SQUEAL: Squeal…

TASH: Right… Squeal?

SQUEAL: Yeah.

TASH: Weird.

SQUEAL: As in pig.

TASH: Let's try and keep the magic shall we… (*Beat.*) How did you…?

SQUEAL: I was in the pub and someone said party at…

TASH: (*Pointing to self.*) Veronica's.

SQUEAL: Veronica's.

TASH: My name.

SQUEAL: Liar.

TASH: You been reading my post?

SQUEAL: Only the junk mail, *Veronica*.

TASH: Keep your snout out, *Squeal*.

> (*TASH lights a fag. Opens the window and perches on the sill. He stares at her. Too long.*)

SQUEAL: (*Gesturing to fridge.*) Some of the stuff in here.

TASH: Don't tell me…

SQUEAL: What do you live on…

TASH: High finance.

SQUEAL: Yeah?

TASH: I'm actually a broker. There's only two women on our board of directors and you're looking at one of them.

SQUEAL: You never would have –

TASH: I don't look the type do I? I hate the way people make assumptions. Air Nike trainers, you must be Soho in media; suit, shirt and matching metallic tie, you're something stylish in high finance. It's all a load of…

SQUEAL: …guessed –

TASH: …bollocks. You know what I mean. And then everyone thinks why then has she never got any money –

SQUEAL: …considering everything that you said last –

TASH: …but it costs a fortune to buy anywhere in London even if it is in some rundown Kosher ghetto with no tube line and a hiding to –

SQUEAL: …last night…Tash –

(TASH is finally silenced.)

We didn't do anything.

(Silence.)

TASH: You can go home now.

SQUEAL: Nothing last night. Alright? Okay?

(A long silence. SQUEAL stares at her. Too long.)

Fine.

(SQUEAL exits. TASH stubs her fag out on the window sill, thinking on this.)

TASH: *(Calling out to him.)* You take it too seriously.

(SQUEAL comes back, dressed and putting his shoes on.)

You need to work at the pump 'em and dump 'em bit.

(SQUEAL continues to ignore her.)

(A long beat.) Nothing?

SQUEAL: Nothing.

TASH: *(Beat.)* I'm glad. *(Seeing his face.)* I don't mean to…

SQUEAL: It's nice to meet someone so –

TASH: Honest.

SQUEAL: It's not as if we're – fourteen –

TASH: I wish.

SQUEAL: You're making me feel –

TASH: Say it.

SQUEAL: (*Beat.*) …like not asking you for that second date.

(*As SQUEAL reaches for his coat, zipping it up and getting ready to go.*)

TASH: Yuri Gagarin. First man on the moon. I remember.

(*SQUEAL continues to get ready, reaching for a motorbike helmet.*)

And then we talked about oceans of water in the space between stars, the kind of soppy bollocks you talk. Squeal is that really your name?

SQUEAL: Yes. Most people call me –

TASH: (*Cutting in.*) And –

SQUEAL: And?

TASH: And you told me about trying to get in the RAF as a fighter pilot at seventeen only they found out you were colour blind and green and red are pretty bloody important if you're going to stop or go and miss a mountain. The joke about the mountain, it was funny. And you cried for a week and I said… 'Great pull line, get the girl every time…' See. I don't forget. Then after the party…which was wild…you came on to me… I fought you off… You said when are we going to fuck. I burst into tears. My mate, Hen said… I looked like white trailer trash but it was a fucking fantastic party… Wasn't it?

SQUEAL: I was in the pub and someone said, 'Party at Veronica's.' But you weren't going. So I hung about and we came back and we talked and you drank and…

TASH: And?

SQUEAL: That's it. No fucking fantastic party. (*Beat.*) Do you want to go out with me again?

TASH: No.

SQUEAL: Right.

TASH: I'll make some tea.

SQUEAL: Milk's off.

(*TASH goes over and opens the fridge.*)

TASH: Have a drink.

SQUEAL: No thanks.

TASH: Have something. You don't have to go.

SQUEAL: What else is there?

TASH: Stay.

SQUEAL: Is this what you do? I stay, you want me to leave. I leave, you try to keep the conversation going.

TASH: Hey, we've just met.

SQUEAL: And you think I'm a mug.

TASH: I don't.

SQUEAL: Yeah you do. That's fine. A one night stand is fine but –

TASH: But?

SQUEAL: I liked last night. Why don't we –

TASH: No. I like it like this. Have breakfast?

SQUEAL: You don't eat it.

TASH: I could make an exception.

SQUEAL: You started this.

TASH: Where?

SQUEAL: On a train.

TASH: Tube.

SQUEAL: It's dangerous, I could have been…

TASH: I started this on a tube…

SQUEAL: On a tube giving me the eye…

TASH: That is a matter of opinion.

SQUEAL: Giving me the eye…

TASH: A matter of…

SQUEAL: …and wanting me to follow you.

(*A long beat.*)

It was a long walk to that pub. I didn't just go for a drink.

TASH: You enjoyed. I thought you enjoyed…

SQUEAL: The intimacy of strangers?

TASH: Stay and we'll have some tea and –

SQUEAL: We'll talk about planets and things we care about and I'll make you laugh and some time very probably as we're really sobering up, you'll cry and I might get a feel and for a moment I'll be everything you want –

(*SQUEAL stops himself saying something.*)

TASH: (*Beat.*) You've done this before?

(*Silence.*)

SQUEAL: Look at yourself.

(*He exits.*)

TASH: Thanks for nothing… (*Calling after him.*) And then what?

(*TASH watches him go; goes to the fridge, takes out the milk, sniffs it.*)

From

SCENES FROM THE BACK OF BEYOND

by Meredith Oakes

This play was first performed at the Royal Court Jerwood Theatre Upstairs, London, in November 2006.

Bill lives in a new Sydney suburb at the end of the 1950s. He is a forty-something scientist who believes the world is improving and that the only thing the human race needs to do is learn. However, his world is turned upside down when one of his neighbours, DAVID, a forty year old atomic scientist who is separated from his wife, spends time in his house. DAVID ends up sleeping with Bill's fifteen year old daughter, JASMINE.

DAVID/JASMINE

DAVID: Oh God!

    Oh God

    What have I done

JASMINE: It's all right

DAVID: You didn't tell me you were / a

JASMINE: What did you think I was?

DAVID: I suppose I just thought kids these days are –

    How old are you?

JASMINE: Fifteen

DAVID: Oh God

JASMINE: I just wanted to lose it

DAVID: You're fifteen

JASMINE: I was waiting for the right person

DAVID: Who

JASMINE: You

DAVID: Jasmine, I don't think we should rush into anything

JASMINE: It's a bit of a strange time to say that

DAVID: I couldn't stop

    I should have stopped

    Why didn't you stop me?

JASMINE: I didn't think you wanted me to stop you.

DAVID: Was it all right

JASMINE: Yeah

    I'll get used to it

DAVID: This shouldn't have happened

JASMINE: What do you mean?

DAVID: I'm your parents' generation

    Not that I want to be

I can't tell you how glad I am to be out of all that mess

But I'm not exactly young and handsome

JASMINE: It doesn't matter

DAVID: Thanks

JASMINE: Other things are more important

DAVID: Yes

What things

JASMINE: Compatibility

DAVID: What

JASMINE: I'm going to be a geologist

DAVID: Oh

Wonderful

JASMINE: I've collected rocks ever since I was a kid

DAVID: Have you

JASMINE: Dad showed me

Dad would have liked to be a geologist really

And when I was little he's say something to me like, 'This is chalcedony', and I'd think, wow, this is chalcedony

You know how kids are

DAVID: I'm trying to think of you as a geologist

JASMINE: But I've always taken more after Dad

DAVID: What would you do about field trips?

You can't make a career in geology without going out on field trips

JASMINE: I go fossicking with Dad sometimes or out where someone's dynamiting something and we can pick up some samples. I like being out in the bush. I can cook damper and everything. Dad and I have walked in the Blue Mountains. People die there. It's so beautiful. The gullies are so deep and cool and the trees are gigantic

DAVID: It's just that men in the circumstances of a field trip tend to be pretty free and easy. I don't know if they'd welcome having a woman along. From the point of view of decency

Jasmine, I could be arrested

This can't happen again

JASMINE: Don't you want it to?

DAVID: It's not that

Please

Jasmine

What would your father say?

JASMINE: He wouldn't mind

He likes you

DAVID: He wouldn't like me if he could see us now

From

BREATHING CORPSES
by Laura Wade

The first performance of Breathing Corpses *took place at the Royal Court Jerwood Theatre Upstairs in London in February 2005.*

Breathing Corpses takes its title from Sophocles' assertion: 'When a man has lost all happiness, he is not alive. Call him a breathing corpse.' The play follows a gruesome cycle of linked deaths and how they affect the living. AMY is a nineteen year old chambermaid in a mid-price hotel. She has a habit of discovering dead bodies in the hotel rooms so when she finds CHARLIE asleep in bed when she enters to clean, she thinks it's happened again. CHARLIE is thirty and described as 'disarmingly attractive'. There is a strong attraction between the two of them but little does AMY know that CHARLIE isn't all that he seems. He may have a Porsche convertible but also a very, very sharp knife.

AMY/CHARLIE

(*AMY comes into the room with clean towels over her arm and a plastic carry-case of cleaning fluids.*

She stops short when she sees the figure in the bed.)

AMY: Oh god, sorry.

(*She goes to back out of the room, then stops again. She turns back slowly for a longer look at the figure in the bed.*)

Right.

God not again.

(*She looks away. Bites her lip.*)

You're supposed to put the Do Not Disturb on. Then I wouldn't come barging in.

(*AMY takes a deep breath and goes over to the bed. She lifts the sheet and looks under it.*

Suddenly the figure moves, sits up, shouts, jumps out of bed. This is CHARLIE. He's just wearing boxer shorts.

AMY gasps, backs away.)

CHARLIE: Who the fuck are / you?

AMY: Shit *fuck* sorry –

(*AMY backs away to the door.*)

Shit.

(*She leans against the door, her hand to her mouth, looking at CHARLIE. He's disarmingly attractive.*)

Sorry.

CHARLIE: What the fuck are you –

AMY: Sorry, house-housekeeping. You didn't put the – You didn't put the Do Not Disturb sign on I – And –

CHARLIE: What, you normally come and lift the sheets off people, did – Did you not see me? (*Looks at his watch.*)

Shit –

AMY: What?

CHARLIE: Missed my alarm.

(*CHARLIE picks up his alarm clock.*)

Didn't set my alarm.

(*He looks at AMY. Sees she's still flattened against the door. Puts the clock down and takes a step towards her.*)

God are you –

AMY: I thought you were dead.

CHARLIE: God, I – I mean crikey, that'd be awful, wouldn't it?

AMY: You had the sheet pulled up over you, I –

CHARLIE: I – I – I always do, I –

AMY: I mean it looked –

CHARLIE: Why would you think I was dead?

AMY: Because –

CHARLIE: I mean, it must happen, but –

AMY: It happens quite a lot.

   (*Beat.*)

   Sorry. Come back later.

CHARLIE: It happens to you?

AMY: Sorry?

CHARLIE: It happens to you quite a lot?

AMY: Yes.

CHARLIE: Shit.

AMY: What?

CHARLIE: It, um, sorry, it suddenly occurs to me I'm just standing here in my boxers.

   (*AMY looks away.*)

AMY: Sorry. I'll –

   (*AMY puts her hand on the doorknob, to leave.*)

CHARLIE: No, hang on, wait. Don't –

AMY: Do the other rooms and come back I –

CHARLIE: No, just let me – I – I want to, you know, sort this out, I just think it'd be better if I had trousers on, if you could just –

   (*CHARLIE goes to the wardrobe and opens it, takes out a pair of trousers.*)

If you could just hang on a second –

AMY: You can say at Reception –

CHARLIE: Sorry?

(*CHARLIE pulls the trousers on.*)

AMY: The manager's behind Reception this morning if you want to /
complain.

CHARLIE: I don't. I don't want to complain.

AMY: Really?

CHARLIE: No. Yes, really.

I'm sorry I jumped out of bed shouting, I mean I was I was
alarming, you were just as alarmed as I was / if not more…

AMY: Oh no, it's –

CHARLIE: I mean, if I'd managed to set my alarm for the right time
– If I hadn't got totally sketched last night, completely knocked
myself out –

AMY: Yeah.

CHARLIE: Just missing my alarm – that's what I'm pissed off about,
not about you, you're

(*CHARLIE looks at AMY.*)

God.

AMY: What?

CHARLIE: Nothing.

(*He holds his hand out to shake hers.*)

Charlie.

AMY: Amy.

Hi.

(*She shakes his hand.*)

CHARLIE: Pleasure to meet you.

AMY: Ooh –

CHARLIE: What?

AMY: Warm hands.

(*They smile at each other.*)

From

OTHER HANDS
by Laura Wade

Other Hands *was commissioned as part of Soho Theatre's Writers' Attachment Programme and was first performed at Soho Theatre, London, in February 2006.*

HAYLEY is a thirty year old management consultant, who specialises in reviewing the performance of staff in problematic businesses and, consequently, people lose their jobs because of her. Her boyfriend, Steve, is very different: he's left his job as a computer consultant and is freelancing with only minimal success. Their relationship is in trouble and they start to drift apart. Steve meets Lydia, a freelance client, and HAYLEY develops feelings for GREG, a forty-five year old married man and current client. Then Steve and HAYLEY develop painful problems with their hands (possibly a form of Repetitive Strain Injury) which prevent them from performing even basic tasks and moving on with their lives. This scene between GREG and HAYLEY takes place in a coffee bar and they are sitting facing each other. GREG is drinking a cappuccino and HAYLEY has an iced coffee with a straw. Despite the problems with HAYLEY's hands, their relationship is in the process of moving up to a new level. They are smiling at each other.

HAYLEY/GREG

HAYLEY: Did you know infinity's not the biggest thing anymore?

GREG: No

HAYLEY: They found something bigger

GREG: What?

HAYLEY: Don't know

It was on the train last week, going to Slough or

GREG: Swindon or

HAYLEY: Somewhere fun. And there's some bloke opposite me reading the New Scientist or something and on the front the headline was 'Infinity – not the biggest thing.'

Makes you think, doesn't it?

GREG: Yeah.

HAYLEY: Made me laugh. And I thought about telling you when I saw it, I sort of turned to you as if you were (*She gestures to the space beside her.*)

I wanted to tell you.

So we should get back to the office, really

GREG: You wouldn't like to sit here flirting a bit longer?

HAYLEY: Would you?

GREG: Give me your hand

HAYLEY: I can't

GREG: Why?

HAYLEY: Hurts to move it

GREG: Alright

Imagine I'm holding your hand

HAYLEY: OK

That's

Surprisingly nice

GREG: Surprisingly?

HAYLEY: Nice surprise, I mean

GREG: You like it

HAYLEY: Yeah

GREG: Good

    (*GREG sits back in his chair.*)

    Side of your nose

HAYLEY: Greg

GREG: Tell me that isn't nice

HAYLEY: It's

GREG: Surprisingly nice

HAYLEY: Yeah

GREG: Which side?

    (*HAYLEY closes her eyes, tilts her head to the left slightly.*)

HAYLEY: That side

GREG: There

    Where now?

    (*HAYLEY tilts her head the other way.*)

HAYLEY: That side

GREG: Yes

    There.

    (*HAYLEY leans forward.*)

HAYLEY: What else?

GREG: Your bottom lip

HAYLEY: God

GREG: I want to…suck your bottom lip

HAYLEY: God

GREG: Too much?

HAYLEY: I

    No, not too much

GREG: Sure?

HAYLEY: Just

    New

Feels different

(*Beat.*)

GREG: Hot, isn't it?

(*GREG smiles.*)

HAYLEY: Your face, you're so naughty

GREG: I want to I want to suck your finger

Each one of them in turn and lick the palm of your hand and a line up your arm, pushing your sleeve back a little and lick the inside of your elbow

And I want to put my hand on your stomach, touch your skin

HAYLEY: God

GREG: And

No, your turn

(*Beat.*)

HAYLEY: OK

I want to…run my fingers through the short hair at the back of your neck

GREG: Uh-huh

HAYLEY: Starched line of your shirt collar

And

And slide my hands around your waist, underneath your jacket

Untuck your shirt at the back, run my fingers along

GREG: I want to put my tongue through the holes between the buttons in your shirt

HAYLEY: And you do these tiny little kisses down the side of my neck

GREG: I want to stand behind you, holding you close round your waist so you feel me hard against your arse

HAYLEY: All the time with these tiny little kisses

GREG: And I want to undo the buttons on your shirt, slide it off your shoulders

HAYLEY: Facing me, your eyes and my eyes and your hands in the back of my hair

GREG: And bite your shoulder

HAYLEY: Bite my shoulder?

GREG: Gently. It'll be nice

HAYLEY: Your hands in the back of my hair and stroking my hair

Pulling me to you

GREG: And then undo the button on your trousers and slide the zip down

HAYLEY: Your hands either side of my face

GREG: Slide my hand inside

HAYLEY: Kissing my eyelids

GREG: Before you expect me to

Make you shiver with the surprise

Slide my hand into your pants

HAYLEY: Knickers. God, are we at knickers already?

GREG: I don't know, are we?

(*HAYLEY looks at GREG, thinking. A moment. She bends down slowly to take a sip of her iced coffee. GREG watches her.*)

From

OFF CAMERA
by Marcia Layne

*The first performance of this play took place at the Courtyard
Theatre at the West Yorkshire Playhouse in June 2003.*

ANISHA and Babs are British born girls in their late twenties/
early thirties on holiday in Jamaica. Babs is there to see if there
might be something to her relationship with local man, Passion,
whom she met the previous year, and, ANISHA has a secret and
very personal mission to find her father, who left his family to
return to Jamaica just before ANISHA's tenth birthday. Babs sets
up ANISHA on a date with RAS SIMI, Passion's friend. ANISHA
isn't too happy about it but she goes anyway. She's not so sure
he isn't just another Jamaican gigolo. They meet at a cliff-side
bar at sunset.

ANISHA/RAS SIMI

ANISHA: The view from here is amazing.

RAS SIMI: (*Looking at her.*) Me see dat.

ANISHA: You're so lucky. (*Sees he is looking at her and looks embarrassed.*)

RAS SIMI: Me lucky yes, me see dat too.

> (*ANISHA looks uncomfortable and preoccupies herself with putting the lime on the bites on her arm.*)

ANISHA: I don't know what Babs told you, but I'm not really looking for… I don't want to seem ungrateful…

RAS SIMI: She tell me she hav da rite girl fi me.

ANISHA: Did she now?

RAS SIMI: Say she garn bring yu fram Inglan, come show me.

ANISHA: Is that right? Well, she didn't bring me anywhere. She came on one mission, I came on another and she doesn't know what that is… (*Sees he's smiling and stops.*) What?

RAS SIMI: Joke me a mek man.

ANISHA: Ha ha, very funny.

RAS SIMI: Me like ow yu look wen yu bex dough.

ANISHA: What did she really tell yu?

RAS SIMI: She aks me to take yu sumwhere nice and protect yu from da gigolo dem.

ANISHA: (*Shaking her head.*) Like I can't take care of myself. (*Jokingly.*) Anyway, how do I know you're not one? Someone told me no true rasta would live here.

RAS SIMI: Who tell yu dat?

ANISHA: A true rasta. (*Smiles.*) Just someone I met.

RAS SIMI: Fus ting, me nah live yah, me jus wuk.

ANISHA: Where do you live?

RAS SIMI: In da ills. Nex ting, ow yu no me nat a gigolo? Every fish inna de sea, nuh shark.

ANISHA: I was just joking.

RAS SIMI: A serious ting man. Camouflage dread a run up an dung wearin dem fashion locks fi get ooman but dem nah read a psalm yet or study heny of de teachins of Jah.

ANISHA: So you read the bible.

RAS SIMI: Yes man, me read Psalm 37 afta me lost me fare dis marning. Fret not dyself becah a evildoers, ah be (*Pauses.*) sumting bout de worker of iniquity rar rar rar and den me run me taxi til me ready fe link yu and mek back some of me money. So ow me no yu nat one a dem touris oo jus wan sample da big bamboo an den bruk a man art?

ANISHA: (*Smiling.*) That's exactly what I am.

RAS SIMI: Well mi art ready fi mash. Come nuh baby.

ANISHA: You really get women like that?

RAS SIMI: Yeah man, ow yu mean? Mi jus ear bout one fram Canada, one week she dideh and seven man she hav.

ANISHA: She's good man, I'd have taken Sunday off.

RAS SIMI: Yu a Christian?

ANISHA: Ish. I was raised an Aventist.

RAS SIMI: Yuh sabbat Sataday den?

ANISHA: I haven't practised for years. I still believe in God but I don't go to church anymore. I haven't been since I was a child.

RAS SIMI: White man use da church tu brainwash de African min'. Jamaica full a dem an look wha gwan.

ANISHA: You know a teacher once told me when the English came into Africa, they had the bible and we had the land. They said kneel down and close your eyes and then they had the land, we had the bible.

RAS SIMI: Si it deh. Only Nigeria have more church dan yah and dem no betta off dan we. Wha Marley say now, (*Sings.*) emancipate yuhself fram mental slavery, none but ourself can free our min'.

ANISHA: That's my favourite song by Bob Marley, that one and Zimbabwe.

RAS SIMI: Yu know bout reggae music den?

ANISHA: I was born in England but that don't make me English.

RAS SIMI: Wha mek?

ANISHA: Is it your place of birth which defines you or your culture and your heritage? My parents were born here and I was raised (*Patois.*) wid ackee and sa'fish, rice and peas, soup pon Saturday, yam, green banana, cho cho, okra, snapper, mango, roast breadfruit, curry goat, reggae, lovers rock, rars and every udda claat known to man.

RAS SIMI: Bumba.

ANISHA: Dat one too. It didn't feel right when you called me a tourist earlier. I wasn't born here but I feel Jamaican.

RAS SIMI: How dat feel?

ANISHA: I feel like…like I've come home.

RAS SIMI: Member say yuh an African Queen. Africa is da true homeland of all black people.

ANISHA: I've never been to Africa so I don't know but this feels right to me. It's not a physical thing…it's kind of I…guess it's spiritual.

RAS SIMI: Welcome home den Empress.

ANISHA: (*Smiling.*) Thank you.

From

THINGS YOU SHOULDN'T SAY PAST MIDNIGHT

by Peter Ackerman

Things You Shouldn't Say Past Midnight *was originally produced in New York and was first performed in the United Kingdom as a rehearsed reading, produced by Old Vic New Voices and Soho Theatre Company. The first performance was at Soho Theatre in November 2002.*

Six characters from wildly different backgrounds make love, war and hysteria in three different beds late one night in Manhattan. GRACE is a sexually adventurous art historian who is spending time with GENE, a New York Italian hitman who works for Dutch mobsters. His brother Mark is GRACE's therapist and she met him at a friend's party. GRACE is turned on by what she perceives to be GENE's tough-man image but he's actually much more sensitive and straight-laced than she bargained for.

GENE/GRACE

GENE: Don't you want to be with someone better than you?

GRACE: No. I want to be with you! Now rip me to pieces!

GENE: But I always wanted to be with someone more educated than me, so I could elevate myself. Don't you feel that?

GRACE: Well I guess eventually it would be nice to be with someone smart.

(*GENE looks demolished.*)

Oh no, Gene, I didn't mean it that way. You're smart. Really. Very smart. Don't obsess about the college thing. It's stupid. Really. See, this is why we shouldn't talk. You're great, Gene. All the things Mark has told me are true, the way you got a job, took care of him, put him through college. That's smart.

GENE: I didn't have a choice.

GRACE: And that's the adult reaction. You did what you had to do.

GENE: I wish I went to college and Mark was the hitman.

GRACE: Maybe he'd be Clean Mark the Killing Machine.

GENE: I don't thinks so.

GRACE: But you're Clean Gene!

GENE: Yeah.

GRACE: And everyone's afraid of Clean Gene.

GENE: Sort of.

GRACE: What do you mean 'sort of'?

GENE: They don't take the Dutch seriously.

GRACE: They're Mafia!

GENE: But they're not Italian. My boss's name is Rut. (*Pronounced 'Root'.*) Who ever heard of a Mafia Don named Rut?

GRACE: There's Dutch Schultz.

GENE: He was big time. My guys are small. There's only three of them. Rut, Hecka Herrit and Jap. (*Pronounced 'Yawp'.*)

GRACE: You're Italian.

GENE: I know, but I didn't make it at first with the Garbolenies, so the Italian guys don't think I deserve it.

GRACE: Who says that?

GENE: I hear it around.

GRACE: You tell me which ones.

GENE: No. It's stupid. I'm just saying I'm not as tough as you make me out.

GRACE: Are you kidding? When I saw you at Mimi's party I said, 'Who is that tough guy?' I couldn't figure out what you were doing at that party.

GENE: I whacked Mimi's brother.

GRACE: You see? Every second I interview for a dumb advertising-sticker job, you are out on the street making life and death decisions. Do you not appreciate the gravity of what you do?

GENE: Yeah, but I don't decide who gets whacked. I just whack 'em. And it's routine, you know? I've got my thing.

GRACE: The plastic bag.

GENE: Yeah, the plastic bag. I tie 'em up, plastic bag 'em, leave the room, and five minutes later they're blue. No muss, no fuss.

GRACE: Clean Gene the Killing Machine.

GENE: Yeah, but it gets old.

GRACE: No, Gene. Don't say that. Why would you say that?

GENE: It's been building up.

GRACE: Don't be a snivelling boy.

GENE: I'm not. I'm trying to tell you something.

GRACE: I don't want to hear it, Gene. Play your strong hand.

GENE: But you get me thinking, Grace.

GRACE: Well don't. What did you do today?

GENE: I don't want to talk about it.

GRACE: Why not?

GENE: I don't like it.

GRACE: I do.

GENE: Don't say that.

GRACE: You don't want to talk about my two favourite subjects, murder and sex.

GENE: Shh! Don't say that!

GRACE: Even the words?

GENE: I like to talk about things I can't do or don't do, 'cause I don't get the chance to do 'em.

GRACE: Okay, fine. So let's just do it, if that's what you like.

GENE: Yeah. That's what I like.

GRACE: (*Sexy.*) What do you like?

GENE: I like to just…

GRACE: Yeah?

GENE: Lemme turn out the light.

GRACE: No! Don't turn out the light! Talk to me.

GENE: I thought you liked me 'cause I don't talk.

GRACE: About certain things, Gene, like 'what are you going to do with the rest of your life.' That doesn't interest me, okay? I wanna fuck and fight, and talk about whacking and sex.

GENE: Yeah, but I'm…

GRACE: What?

GENE: …thinking of making a change.

GRACE: What kind of change?

GENE: A job change.

GRACE: Geeeene!!!

GENE: What?

GRACE: You are the only hitman I've ever slept with! Do you have any clue how fucking sexy that is?!!

GENE: Is that why you're with me? 'Cause I'm a hitman?

GRACE: No, baby, I'm with you 'cause you're…well…yeah.

From

A MATTER OF LIFE AND DEATH

*adapted by Tom Morris and Emma Rice
(based on the film by Michael Powell and
Emeric Pressburger)*

*This adaptation was first performed in May 2007
at the National Theatre, London in association with
Kneehigh Theatre.*

A Matter of Life and Death is based on the 1946 film and tells
the story of a pilot (PETER) who bails out of a Lancaster bomber
in May 1945 without a parachute and miraculously survives
following an angelic blunder. Before he jumps, PETER is in
contact with a radio telephone operator, JUNE, and afterwards
goes to find her. Of course they fall in love. However, it isn't all
happy endings as Peter finds himself in a heavenly court, fighting
for his survival on earth. This scene is part of the opening of the
play when Peter is in his burning plane. He holds a radio: two
tin cans connected with red string. He throws one end into the
air and JUNE catches it.

JUNE/PETER

JUNE: Are you receiving me? Request your position! Come in, Lancaster!

PETER: I like your voice. I can't give you my position. Instruments gone. Crew gone too. Except Bob, my Sparks. He's dead. The others baled out. On my orders. Time 03:35. Got that?

JUNE: Three crew dead. Three baled out – 03:35!

PETER: They'll be sorry about Bob. We all liked him.

(*Burst of interference.*)

JUNE: Hello! G George! Hello! G George! Are you alright? Are you going to try to land? Do you want a fix?

PETER: The name's not 'G for George', it's 'P for Peter'. Peter D Carter. D's for David. Squadron Leader Peter Carter. No, I'm not landing. Undercarriage is gone. Port engine's on fire. I am baling out presently. I am baling out. Take a telegram!

JUNE: Got your message! Received your message. We can hear you.

PETER: Telegram to my mother. Mrs Ray Carter, 88 Hampstead Lane, London, North West.

JUNE: 88 Hampstead Lane, London.

PETER: Tell her that I love her. You'll have to write it for me. What I want her to know is that I love her very much – that I've never shown it to her – not really – but that I've loved her always. Give love to my two sisters too. Don't forget them.

JUNE: Received your message. We can hear you. Are you wounded? Repeat. Are you wounded? Are you baling out?

PETER: What's your name?

JUNE: June.

PETER: June, I am baling out. I am baling out. But there's a catch. I've got no parachute.

(*Burst of interference.*)

JUNE: Hello! Hello Peter! Do not understand. Hello! Hello Peter. Can you hear me?

PETER: Hello June. Don't be afraid. It's quite simple. We've had it! And I'd rather jump than fry. After the first thousand feet what's the difference? I shan't know anything – I say – I hope I haven't frightened you?

JUNE: No! I'm not frightened.

PETER: Good.

JUNE: Your Sparks, you said he was dead. Hasn't he got a 'chute?

PETER: Cut to ribbons. Cannon-shell. June. Are you pretty?

JUNE: Not bad.

PETER: What's your favourite story?

JUNE: *The Wizard of Oz.*

PETER: Best film ever! I wish I had my ruby slippers with me now.

JUNE: So do I.

PETER: Can you hear me as well as I hear you?

JUNE: Yes.

PETER: You have a good voice. You've got guts, too… It's funny. I've known dozens of girls – I was in love with some of them – but a girl whom I've never seen and never shall see, will hear my last words. I say, June, if you're around when they pick me up – turn your head away!

JUNE: No Peter!

We'll find somewhere you can try to land. Wait!

PETER: Don't go June. I'm badly on fire. She might break up at any minute. There's no way I could land.

JUNE: Let me try!

PETER: No. Let me do this in my own way. I want to be alone with you… Are you in love with anybody? No! Don't answer that!

JUNE: I could love a man like you, Peter.

PETER: I love you, June. You're Life and I'm leaving you! Where do you live? On the station?

JUNE: No. In a big country house. About five miles from here. Near the sea. Lee Wood House.

PETER: Old house?

JUNE: Yes. Very old.

PETER: Good. I'll be a ghost and come and see you. You aren't frightened of ghosts are you? It would be awful if you were.

JUNE: I'm not frightened.

PETER: What time will you be home.

JUNE: I'm on duty 'til six. I have breakfast in the mess. Then I have to cycle half an hour. I often go along the sands – oh, this is such nonsense!

PETER: No it isn't. It's the best sense I ever heard. I was lucky to get you, June. It can't be helped about the parachute. But I'll have wings soon anyway. Big white ones. I hope they haven't gone modern yet. I'd hate to have a propeller instead of wings. I say June.

JUNE: Yes.

PETER: Do you think there is anything after this? What do you think the Other world is like? I've got my own ideas –

JUNE: Oh – Peter…

PETER: I think it starts where this one leaves off; or where this one could leave off if we listened to Plato and Aristotle and Jesus; with all our little earthly problems solved but with greater problems worth the solving – I'll know soon enough. I'm signing off now June. Goodbye! Goodbye June.

(*Burst of interference.*)

JUNE: Hello G for George. Hello G George. Hello G George.

(*PETER throws his radio out of the plane and he prepares to jump.*)

From

CRESSIDA AMONG THE GREEKS
by David Foley

Cressida Among the Greeks *was first performed at the Ohio Theatre in New York City in February 2002.*

This play is an updated version of Shakespeare's *Troilus and Cressida* and explores love and betrayal amidst the chaos of war. TROILUS, a Trojan Prince, is barely twenty years old and in love with the older CRESSIDA. The city of Troy, in which they live, is under siege from the Greek army so emotions are running high. CRESSIDA's father, the Trojan priest Calchas who defected over to the Greek side, organises for CRESSIDA to be exchanged for a Trojan prisoner of war. A Greek Lord, Diomedes, escorts her across the battle lines against her will. Distraught and lonely in the Greek camp, CRESSIDA eventually succumbs to Diomedes, despite still loving Troilus. When Troilus secretly steals into the Greek camp, desperate to see CRESSIDA, he finds her in the arms of his rival.

CRESSIDA/TROILUS

(*Outside CRESSIDA's tent. Near dawn. TROILUS enters. He is smeared with dirt. A scratch across his face, clothes torn. He gazes a moment at the tent, then moves to the tent flap and hisses through it.*)

TROILUS: Cressida! Cressida! (*There's no answer. He falls to his knees, exhausted, almost sobbing.*) Cressida please! Answer me! Cressida!

CRESSIDA: (*Sleepily, from inside the tent.*) Who's there?

TROILUS: It's me. It's Troilus. I'm here. Let me in.

CRESSIDA: (*Coming from the tent.*) God! Troilus! (*She kneels and takes his face in her hands.*) What are you doing here? How did you get here?

TROILUS: I don't know. I don't know. I walked from Troy. Three leagues. I crawled through brambles. I slipped the sentries. I don't know how. I asked a servant girl where your tent was. That's it. That's all. I'm here.

CRESSIDA: I can see that. But why? I mean, good God! It's so dangerous!

TROILUS: What does it matter? I'm here. Aren't you glad?

(*He kisses her but she barely responds.*)

What's the matter?

(*She strokes his cheek in tender perplexity. He takes her hand and kisses it, then kisses her arm, then her throat, while she helplessly protests.*)

CRESSIDA: Troilus… Don't… Please…

(*He kisses her, and for a moment they kiss passionately.*)

TROILUS: (*Murmurs.*) Take me inside…

CRESSIDA: No.

TROILUS: No? Why not?

CRESSIDA: Troilus, I want you to go.

TROILUS: Go…?

CRESSIDA: Listen! It's dangerous for you to be here. If they catch you, they'll kill you. It'll be light soon. You won't find it so easy to cross the lines in daylight.

TROILUS: It doesn't matter. I'll stay with you. They won't find me inside your tent.

CRESSIDA: Troilus, no. Now listen. Maybe we can find a guard, someone we can bribe, someone to guide you past the sentries.

TROILUS: Why are you saying this? Don't you want me here?

CRESSIDA: I'm trying to save your skin, my love. Your precious, lovely skin.

(*He kisses her again. After a moment, an awkward, weighted stillness rises between them.*)

TROILUS: Why can't I?

CRESSIDA: Why can't you what?

TROILUS: Why can't I go inside?

(*Pause. She meets his eyes.*)

CRESSIDA: Because you can't.

TROILUS: Because…

CRESSIDA: (*Painfully.*) Troilus…

(*He covers his face with his hands.*)

TROILUS: Tell me no. Tell me it's not true.

CRESSIDA: Stop it, Troilus.

TROILUS: (*Looking up at her.*) Tell me it's a lie! *Tell me*!

(*A long silence.*)

Why?

CRESSIDA: I don't know…why.

TROILUS: You don't?

CRESSIDA: (*Sharply.*) No! I don't! How could I?

TROILUS: You betrayed me and you don't know why!

CRESSIDA: Betrayed you? Well…if you say so.

TROILUS: Doesn't it matter to you?

CRESSIDA: Why should it matter? Haven't you noticed the world's turned upside down? There's nothing but betrayal nowadays. We betray each other as we breathe.

TROILUS: I didn't betray *you*!

CRESSIDA: No?

TROILUS: No!

CRESSIDA: Then where were you?

TROILUS: Where was…?

CRESSIDA: When all my hopes collapsed around me and I was scattered to the wind – where were you?

TROILUS: I…

CRESSIDA: You left me on my own, my dear. What was I to do?

TROILUS: (*Abashed.*) I – I – couldn't…

CRESSIDA: No, of course you couldn't. There was nothing to be done. That's my point exactly.

TROILUS: But I never betrayed our love! I was faithful to you!

CRESSIDA: I don't even know what that means.

TROILUS: It means I didn't throw our love away the moment you were out of sight. Or did you never love me?

CRESSIDA: Love you? *Love* you? God! Like a prisoner's last day of sunlight! Like everything I've ever wanted and everything I've lost! I loved you – as my last, best hope on earth. But so what? Really, Troilus, *so what*?

TROILUS: How can you –

CRESSIDA: Look at us, Troilus. Where do we stand? There isn't a common square of earth to hold us. I'm an exile and a refugee. My fate is tied here – where I stand. And here you're an enemy. Every minute you remain exposes you to murder.

TROILUS: Cressida –

CRESSIDA: We lost, Troilus. It's over. There's nothing left for us. So go away! Go back to Troy! Maybe there's a chance for you there. Because there isn't any here. Why stand here torturing me? So we can add *your* corpse to that huge and senseless pile?

(*Pause.*)

TROILUS: I'll go. If you come with me.

CRESSIDA: What – ?

(*He seizes her arm.*)

TROILUS: Yes, yes! You said it yourself. You have no home in Troy, and I can't stay here. So we'll leave them both behind us. We'll ride out together and take our chances in the world. We'll follow stars and take strange roads and find ourselves – somewhere – a home.

CRESSIDA: Troilus –

TROILUS: Come with me!

(*He takes her in his arms. They kiss hungrily. She clings to him, and for a moment they are lost in a furious ecstasy, as if they really have left everything behind them. He murmurs softly, 'Come with me, come with me, come with me, come with me…' She murmurs dazedly, 'Yes, yes, yes…' Finally, she breaks away.*)

(*A gentle plea.*) Come with me…

(*She has turned away from him, her face in her hands.*)

What's wrong?

(*She turns to him with a stricken, mortified gaze.*)

CRESSIDA: Oh, Troilus… I can't.

TROILUS: You –

CRESSIDA: I can't. I can't.

TROILUS: Why not? Why can't you – ?

CRESSIDA: Think what's out there. Think of the brutal, empty waste beyond the world we know. The untamed land. The savage tribes.

TROILUS: I'll be there with you. I'll protect you.

CRESSIDA: Troilus, I'm not that brave. I can't face monsters. Dragons. Bands of brigands. I can't starve or sleep in forests or fend off wolves. I'm not – that brave.

TROILUS: Then you don't love me after all.

CRESSIDA: (*Hopelessly.*) Oh, yes. I do. Just not enough.

(*She covers her face. In sudden anger, he strikes her down with the back of his hand. She falls to the ground.*)

TROILUS: *I'll kill him!*

CRESSIDA: *What?*

TROILUS: That man in there. This is his fault. He changed you. He stole you from me. Let him come out! Let him face me!

CRESSIDA: (*Scrambling to her feet.*) Don't!

From

CAMILLE by Neil Bartlett
(adapted from *La Dame aux caméllias*
by Alexandre Dumas *fils*)

Camille *opened at the Lyric Hammersmith, London, in*
March 2003.

Set in nineteenth century Paris, *Camille* follows the story of
MARGUERITE GAUTIER, otherwise known as 'La Dame aux
camellias' in Alexandre Dumas' novel of the same name.
MARGUERITE is the most beautiful, glamorous and expensive
prostitute in town. ARMAND DUVAL falls in love with her on their
first meeting and, as MARGUERITE struggles with tuberculosis
and the thought of death, the obsession becomes mutual. In
this scene, ARMAND and MARGUERITE negotiate their first night
together.

MARGUERITE/ARMAND

MAGUERITE: You say it was love / at first sight –

ARMAND: I was very rude the first time we met, and / I thought –

MAGUERITE: Yes, you were – but apparently this great love of yours
didn't stop you going home and getting a good night's sleep –

ARMAND: Well that's where you're wrong.

Do you remember the night we met?

MAGUERITE: No.

ARMAND: I do. After you left the Opéra Comique at eleven, you
walked to the Café de Anglais, and you stayed there until just
before one in the morning. When you came out, I followed your
carriage; it brought you back here, and I watched you get out, on
your own, unlock the door, and come inside; on your own. The
fact that you were on your own made me very happy. I then spent
the entire night standing underneath your window.

(*MARGUERITE has started laughing.*)

What's so funny?

MAGUERITE: Nothing – there was a very good reason why I was on
my own.

ARMAND: Which was?

MAGUERITE: Someone was expecting me.

ARMAND: Goodbye.

MAGUERITE: I knew you'd be angry; why do men always insist on
being told what they don't want to know?

ARMAND: Oh I can assure you Madam that I'm not at all angry. It
was entirely natural that someone should have been waiting for
you at half past one in the morning, just as it is entirely natural for
me to be leaving at the same hour.

MAGUERITE: Why, is someone expecting you?

(*Beat.*)

ARMAND: Why do you want to hurt me?

MAGUERITE: Who on earth do you think you are talking to? I don't
have to account for my actions to you. If you're going to get

jealous and make scenes before we've even started, what on earth will it be like when we –

If we –

I've never met a man like you.

ARMAND: That's because no man has ever loved you like I love you.

MAGUERITE: Ha!

How long?

ARMAND: Ever since I first saw you get out of your carriage and go into Susse and Sons wearing a white cashmere shawl.

MAGUERITE: And what am I supposed to do with this great love of yours?

ARMAND: Love me back.

MAGUERITE: What about the Duke?

ARMAND: What Duke?

MAGUERITE: My Duke. The rich, jealous one.

ARMAND: He won't find out.

MAGUERITE: And if he does?

ARMAND: He'll forgive you.

MAGUERITE: No he won't, he'll leave me.

ARMAND: You're already risking that.

MAGUERITE: How do you know that?

ARMAND: From the way you gave Nanine instructions to say that you weren't at home tonight.

MAGUERITE: Yes but that particular customer's a very valued one.

ARMAND: Not that valued if you lock him out at this hour of the morning.

MAGUERITE: Are you complaining about the fact that my door's locked…?

(*He has got closer during above; he takes her round the waist.*)

ARMAND: God I love you.

MAGUERITE: How much?

ARMAND: I swear –

MAGUERITE: If you promise to do everything I ever ask of you without saying a word –

ARMAND: I'll do anything –

MAGUERITE: Without asking me to justify the slightest detail –

ARMAND: Anything –

(*Break.*)

MAGUERITE: We'll see.

ARMAND: When will we see?

MAGUERITE: Later.

ARMAND: Why not now?

MAGUERITE: Because… (*She puts a red camellia in his buttonhole.*)…you can't always take possession on the day you sign the contract.

ARMAND: When am I going to see you again?

MAGUERITE: When this camellia turns white.

ARMAND: And when will that be?

MAGUERITE: Tomorrow night, starting at midnight and ending at half past one. Satisfied?

ARMAND: What do you think?

From

UNDER THE BLACK FLAG
by Simon Bent

Under the Black Flag *was first performed at Shakespeare's Globe, London in July 2006.*

Under the Black Flag is subtitled *The Early Life, Adventures and Pyracies of the Famous Long John Silver Before He Lost His Leg.* Based on the character in *Treasure Island* and transplanted to the time of Cromwell's Commonwealth, the story explores how LONG JOHN SILVER came to piracy and ended up a legend. This scene takes place in Rabat-Sale, Morocco, where the pirates are now based. ISABELLE is the mistress of pirate captain, Kees de Keyser. Kees not only lost his power to JOHN SILVER in a kind of pirate parliament but also ISABELLE's affection. However, she is extremely jealous of SILVER's feeling for the Sultan's daughter, which ultimately leads her to betray him.

SILVER/ISABELLE

SILVER: Declare yourself.

ISABELLE: Sir.

SILVER: Isabelle.

ISABELLE: In the dark.

SILVER: I pray.

ISABELLE: You are returned ahead of the others.

SILVER: We attacked two bullion ships, The Adventurer and The Charity. But after we had strung up their captains and set about murdering their crews, those ships resembled more a hospital or slaughterhouse, and I could not bear to inflict any more misery. So I let mine go. The Charity. While the others carved up their prey, I let mine go.

ISABELLE: Come to bed.

SILVER: Awhile.

ISABELLE: You pray.

SILVER: Every night – salvation, some sign, every night these last eight years since I first came ashore to Rabat Sale. Eight long years since He laid His hand upon me, since He chose me as His 'pirate saint', since He chose me as His instrument. And every day I have waited for some sign. Eight years. And every day I wake no clearer as to my purpose, nothing changes, I grow older and I descend further. I am a cutthroat.

ISABELLE: Come, my love.

SILVER: It's cold.

ISABELLE: My lover.

SILVER: I'm cold.

ISABELLE: Here. My scarf.

(*She puts scarf round him.*)

You need to sleep.

SILVER: I don't sleep, I can't sleep.

ISABELLE: My love.

(*Strokes his hair.*)

Tell me.

SILVER: Nothing. You have arranged a secret rendezvous for me with the English Ambassador.

ISABELLE: Yes.

SILVER: How can we know to trust him.

ISABELLE: You can't. Tell me.

SILVER: He wants to strike a deal so as I lay off attacking the English ships.

ISABELLE: Why won't you tell me.

SILVER: There's nothing to tell.

ISABELLE: Then nothing shall be your company.

SILVER: No, don't go. I don't sleep, I can't sleep, I have made many enemies, I am a prisoner.

ISABELLE: Is there nowhere safe beyond this fortress.

SILVER: No port, no safe haven.

ISABELLE: There is one place, a place I know that you have taken to going to each day at sunset – the olive grove by the mosque.

SILVER: Oh, not this again.

ISABELLE: You go there without me.

SILVER: It's a good place, a holy place –

ISABELLE: So I'm not allowed to walk there.

SILVER: Safe from prying eyes.

ISABELLE: Hanging around so that you might catch a glimpse of the Sultan's daughter.

SILVER: She walks back that way from prayer and reminds me of my own.

ISABELLE: Nothing more.

SILVER: No.

ISABELLE: She smiles.

SILVER: No.

ISABELLE: Why not, what's she unhappy about.

SILVER: I don't know…oh, alright – yes, sometimes she smiles.

ISABELLE: And you smile back.

SILVER: No.

ISABELLE: Never.

SILVER: No, never, sometimes – by chance.

ISABELLE: You speak.

SILVER: Never.

ISABELLE: But she looks.

SILVER: Sometimes, yes.

ISABELLE: You look back.

SILVER: No, never.

ISABELLE: Then how do you know that she looks.

SILVER: I don't.

ISABELLE: You find her attractive.

SILVER: No.

ISABELLE: Oh. Maybe you prefer boys.

SILVER: Give me strength, why is it – why is it, tell me…you think like a woman.

ISABELLE: I am a woman. You prefer boys.

SILVER: No. I don't.

ISABELLE: You don't find the Sultan's daughter attractive.

SILVER: Alright, she's pretty.

ISABELLE: So you do, you think she's pretty.

SILVER: Yes, I do.

ISABELLE: Yes, she's pretty.

SILVER: Aye.

ISABELLE: Then from now you pay like all the others.

From

LOVE SONG
by John Kolvenbach

Love Song *received its world premiere in March 2006,
produced by Steppenwolf Theatre Company, Chicago. It
received its European premiere in the West End of London at
the New Ambassadors Theatre in November 2006.*

Beane is described as an 'exile from life – an oddball'. His
well-meaning sister JOAN and brother-in-law HARRY try to make
time for him in their busy lives, but no one can get through.
However, when Beane meets his soul-mate, Molly, his world
lights up and he's supremely happy. However, is it love, or
just a figment of his imagination? *Love Song* explores the idea
that sometimes we need fantasies to cope with the stress of
day-to-day life. Beane's new found happiness inspires his sister
and brother-in-law into some extra-curricular love-making of
their own. This scene is set in JOAN and HARRY's apartment: it
is a weekday morning and they are both wearing bathrobes.

Square brackets indicate a change in tone.

JOAN/HARRY

(*JOAN regards the phone.*)

JOAN: I can't do it.

HARRY: You can absolutely do it.

JOAN: I'm a terrible liar.

HARRY: You are a magnificent liar.

JOAN: Am I?

HARRY: Of course you are.

JOAN: What do I *say*?

HARRY: You're sick and you can't come in.

JOAN: Is that all it is?

HARRY: (*Handing JOAN the phone.*) It's a cinch. Here.
(*Pause. JOAN regards the phone.*)

JOAN: You know how many times I've cursed the people who do this?

HARRY: A million?

JOAN: Now here I am doing it, I can't believe it.

HARRY: You're a convert to the world of lying and sloth, – [Jesus
Christ, Jo.]
(*Beat.*)

JOAN: [What?]

HARRY: [*Wow.*]

JOAN: [What.]

HARRY: [Have you *always* had that?]

JOAN: [The robe?]

HARRY: [Where'd you get that?]

JOAN: [I dunno, I stole it from some hotel, why.]

HARRY: [Jesus *Christ.*]

JOAN: [You like it?]

HARRY: [It's not a thing of liking it, it's a thing of The Fucking Robe
Makes My Insides Hurt.]

JOAN: (*Flattered.*) [Get outta town.]

HARRY: [I am not kidding.]

JOAN: [Don't I always wear this?]

HARRY: [It's a thing of the Robe is *Tantalizing*.]

JOAN: [Really?]

HARRY: [It's a thing of what is it *made* of, it's like someone harvested, harvested my *soul* and then took a *loom* and with the fabric, I guess with the fabric of my soul they made a robe, and then there you are wearing my soul except of course technically it's actually still a *robe*.]

(*Beat.*)

JOAN: [Honey, I'm sorry, I'm not sure what that means.]

HARRY: [I got lost halfway through there.]

JOAN: [It got away from you a little bit.]

HARRY: [I'm not used to talking like that, it just sort of ran away from me.]

JOAN: [You like the robe.]

HARRY: [That was my point.]

JOAN: [I got that part.]

HARRY: [That seeing it on you makes me want to take it off you.]

(*Beat.*)

JOAN: [See now that I understand.]

HARRY: [Right?]

JOAN: Gimme that phone, hand that fucking thing over here.

HARRY: (*Handing her the phone.*) You're gonna do it?

JOAN: Yes I am. (*Beat. Handing it back.*) Right after you.

HARRY: You want me to go?

JOAN: It makes me *nervous,* I don't *know* why, It's like I'm cutting *class* and smoking pot and tricking my mother, it is very *Exciting.*

HARRY: (*Dialing.*) [I love this, once a week we should do this, the rest of the world calls in sick every other *day*, we should –] (*Into the phone.*) Kate. (*Then, holding his nose to sound congested.*) Kate, hi it's Harry, listen, I've got this I don't know what it is, something bronchial, it's really terrible. (*Beat.*) Oh you're sweet, could you? That would be great. (*Beat.*) I know, plenty of fluids. (*A fake sneeze.*) (*Beat.*) Thanks, God bless you too. (*HARRY hangs up.*)

(*Beat.*)

JOAN: *Harry.*

HARRY: Right?

JOAN: God bless you too?

HARRY: Was that too much?

JOAN: You blessed her right back.

HARRY: Did that work?

JOAN: and the *sneeze.*

HARRY: Was the sneeze good?

JOAN: Who knew the husband was so talented?

HARRY: (*Handing JOAN the phone.*) Throw one into *your* thing.

JOAN: Should I?

HARRY: *Hell* yes, give it a little panache.

JOAN: [Doesn't this feel like high school?]

HARRY: [I love it.]

JOAN: [We should be smoking cigarettes and making out on the sofa.]

HARRY: [Let's get some cigarettes.]

JOAN: [Who was the first girl you ever kissed?]

HARRY: [You.]

JOAN: [Shut up.]

HARRY: [I saved myself.]

JOAN: (*Dialing.*) [You are so full of malarkey. Me.]

HARRY: Throw the sneeze in there!

JOAN: (*Dialing.*) I'm gonna toss in a whopper, watch this, I am gonna
    sneeze her into *oblivion* – (*Into the phone, holding her nose to sound
    congested.*) Louise? (*Fake sneeze.*) It's me. (*Fake sneeze.*)

HARRY: [Very nice.]

JOAN: (*Into the phone.*) I'm sick.

HARRY: [Sure, great, get right to the point.]

JOAN: (*Into the phone.*) I've got something bad.

HARRY: [Perfect.]

JOAN: (*Into the phone.*) I'm not sure. Something very bad.

From

SILENCE AND VIOLENCE
by Torben Betts

The first production of Silence and Violence *took place at The White Bear Theatre, London in 2002.*

HOLLOWAY is an aristocrat whose husband, WINDERMERE, is a senior officer in the army and away at war. Giesbach, an artist, is beaten by a mob of women who are angry that he refuses to bear arms when their husbands, fathers, brothers and sons face almost certain death in battle. HOLLOWAY uses her influence to save Giesbach from the mob. She then poses naked for a portrait and makes love to him. WINDERMERE returns victorious from the war and is made Governor, whilst Giesbach is arrested for his objection and faces certain death. When HOLLOWAY admits to a night of adultery, WINDERMERE shoots her. Years later, WINDERMERE releases Giesbach from prison to commemorate his wife's beauty in a national monument to be dug out of a cliff face (as a desperate attempt to win back the respect of his people). He asks the artist to use his wife's perfectly preserved body, which he idolises, as inspiration. Little does WINDERMERE know that Giesbach once knew her in the flesh.

This scene focuses on the moment when WINDERMERE arrives home from the war. He is in an excited state, covered in blood and carrying a present about the size of a hat-box, which we later learn contains a severed head.

WINDERMERE/HOLLOWAY

(*HOLLOWAY leaps to her feet.*)

HOLLOWAY: My darling! I'm so glad that you… What has happened to your…?

WINDERMERE: (*Who talks at great speed.*) Missed me?

HOLLOWAY: You know I…

WINDERMERE: Dreamed of you. Nightly. In HQ.

HOLLOWAY: Naturally.

WINDERMERE: Imagined intercourse.

HOLLOWAY: Yes.

WINDERMERE: With you. Too long without grind.

HOLLOWAY: We can soon put that…

WINDERMERE: These days. Army full of arsefuckers.

HOLLOWAY: What has happened to your clothes?

WINDERMERE: My boy. Carried equipment. Made tea. Polished medals. Polished my gun. Old gun. Faulty mechanism. Blew off his face. Standing right by me.

HOLLOWAY: You know you are on public…?

WINDERMERE: Face slid down the wall. Still smiling as it slid. Had just cracked joke about Irish. Funny joke.

HOLLOWAY: The people want your words, darling. You are a…

WINDERMERE: Did you hear news?

HOLLOWAY: And I'm sorry I'm not dressed yet. Your arrival…

WINDERMERE: Governor been caught playing Hide the Sausage with whore.

HOLLOWAY: …was announced scarcely…

WINDERMERE: Think he'll resign. They want me to take over.

HOLLOWAY: Really?

WINDERMERE: When fighting finito.

HOLLOWAY: I thought it was…?

WINDERMERE: Not till they beg us. Beg us for mercy. Should we kiss now?

HOLLOWAY: Yes. Yes, of course.

(*They kiss.*)

WINDERMERE: (*Proffering gift.*) For you.

HOLLOWAY: I know what this is.

WINDERMERE: Don't think so.

HOLLOWAY: It's a hat, hand-crafted by the peasants across the water. They are famous for their dress-making and their…

WINDERMERE: Not quite.

HOLLOWAY: But it is a hat, surely? You always buy me hats. We have had to build another room to accommodate them all. I'll open it after we've…

WINDERMERE: (*Putting box on table.*) Seen outside house?

HOLLOWAY: Yes.

WINDERMERE: Flag-wavers on lawn. Children on gate, climbing on wall. Police getting edgy. Banners and such. 'Captain Windermere, your nation is proud.'

HOLLOWAY: And so is your wife.

WINDERMERE: Killed many thousands.

HOLLOWAY: Yes.

WINDERMERE: Hundreds of thousands.

HOLLOWAY: It's alright.

WINDERMERE: Women and children. Huddled in houses.

HOLLOWAY: That's the nature of…

WINDERMERE: Still love me then?

HOLLOWAY: Yes. Of course I…

WINDERMERE: Press playing game.

HOLLOWAY: We need to change your clothes…

WINDERMERE: Keeping herd diverted.

HOLLOWAY: …if you are to make this speech.

WINDERMERE: Not good with words.

HOLLOWAY: I know you're not.

WINDERMERE: Not good with language.

HOLLOWAY: No.

WINDERMERE: Man of action.

HOLLOWAY: You are.

WINDERMERE: Speech written for me.

HOLLOWAY: Of course.

WINDERMERE: Might stumble over complicated phrases.

HOLLOWAY: We can practice.

WINDERMERE: Be grateful. Have it learned. Took all day.

HOLLOWAY: Lift up your arms.

WINDERMERE: (*Doing so.*) Like to be Governor's wife then?

HOLLOWAY: (*Undressing him.*) Well…

WINDERMERE: Always on display?

HOLLOWAY: I think I should like…

WINDERMERE: Help me govern.

HOLLOWAY: I will do anything to help my…

WINDERMERE: Bit nervous.

HOLLOWAY: Of course you are.

WINDERMERE: Man of action.

HOLLOWAY: Yes.

WINDERMERE: Not words.

HOLLOWAY: That's why you are loved. You act. You are not afraid to…

WINDERMERE: Where is maidgirl?

HOLLOWAY: She had to leave.

WINDERMERE: Why? Good totty. Long legs. Nice little titbuds.

HOLLOWAY: She didn't agree with the invasion. She felt she could no longer remain in our…

WINDERMERE: Shame. Pert arse. Flat belly.

HOLLOWAY: We can easily…

WINDERMERE: Need grind.

HOLLOWAY: Later.

WINDERMERE: Need one now.

HOLLOWAY: You must first address your…

WINDERMERE: Some officers…strict secret this…some officers… away from bitches…turn arsefucker.

HOLLOWAY: You said.

WINDERMERE: Monotonous war.

HOLLOWAY: Really.

WINDERMERE: All maps in HQ. All bombs from air. Blowing up bridges. Targeting dumps. Rarely see whites, the whites of their eyes.

HOLLOWAY: Turn around.

WINDERMERE: Conscripts all bored. Train 'em up. Sit about playing blackjack. Watching rugby in mess. Game shows.

HOLLOWAY: (*Removing his jacket.*) How old was this boy, this…?

WINDERMERE: Flew a few sorties. Dropped some explosives.

HOLLOWAY: Good.

WINDERMERE: Interesting arsenal. But all done by computer. No sense of teamwork.

HOLLOWAY: That's a shame.

WINDERMERE: Like some male bonding.

HOLLOWAY: Listen darling…

WINDERMERE: And so high up. Prefer hands get dirty. See man when I kill him.

HOLLOWAY: I can imagine.

WINDERMERE: But this…turn up, press that, launch missile, village disappear, go home, have beer, watch television.

HOLLOWAY: Well, the less dangerous it is the…

WINDERMERE: Ancestors, digging trenches, going over top, bayonets flashing, screaming, fear, terrible sounds, shells dropping, bullets fizzing, slicing bellies, hand to hand, man to man. Good clean fighting.

HOLLOWAY: Sit down.

WINDERMERE: (*Doing so.*) Inspected some wreckage. Mashed some civilians. Bit disagreeable. Limbs and lungs and broken heads. Clusters. Mark 40. Dropped very many. Toddlers get shredded.

HOLLOWAY: It is the nature of war that…

WINDERMERE: (*Waving hand.*) Make no mention. See boy's blood here? Sad really. One loss: my boy. Cleaning rifle never used. Souvenir rifle. Ancestor's rifle.

HOLLOWAY: (*Untying bootlaces.*) Let's just get these off you.

WINDERMERE: Don't think, darling…don't think things will ever be the same again.

HOLLOWAY: No.

From

THE FOREVER WALTZ
by Glyn Maxwell

The European premiere of The Forever Waltz *was first performed at the Smirnoff Baby Belly, Edinburgh in August 2005.*

MOBILE arrives in the underworld, searching for his ex-lover, EVIE. Unfortunately he can't remember anything about himself or how he arrived at this point. Watts, a mysterious guitar-wielding guide helps him to remember. In this scene, MOBILE remembers EVIE's wedding day, where he couldn't resist turning up to see her and the man she decided to marry. His pain is evident throughout their exchange and it's clear that he still loves her. When EVIE's new husband starts playing the song that was MOBILE and EVIE's song when they were together, MOBILE grabs the wedding cake knife and stabs her to death.

No wonder his mind wanted to forget.

EVIE/MOBILE

EVIE: Oh my lord.

MOBILE: The same.

EVIE: I knew you'd come though.
Life was perfect, it was on the cards.

MOBILE: How could I not? We go back, you and I,
come a long way.

EVIE: We do, we'll always be,
you know –

MOBILE: You know –

EVIE: There'll always be what there was.

MOBILE: That's absolutely true.
There always is what there was. My philosophy.

EVIE: Nobody tried to stop you.

MOBILE: Nobody did.

EVIE: I wouldn't want that.

MOBILE: A smart chap with a gift,
nobody's going to stop me.

EVIE: Nobody could!
Who ever could? It's good to see you, John.
What have you got me there.

MOBILE: Well it's a surprise,
isn't it? Where's the gentleman of the hour?

EVIE: Oh, he's I don't know.

MOBILE: Is he out there?

(*EVIE goes quickly to the window and signals to say 'Don't play, don't play the song'. MOBILE goes to the window. EVIE draws him back.*)

He's musical.

EVIE: Like you!

MOBILE: Just like me.

EVIE: Perhaps that was my fantasy all along,
          to be a rock-star girl, I didn't mind
          who sang the songs!

MOBILE: Is he going to sing a song?

EVIE: Oh I hope not, they're hopeless.

MOBILE: They look like they're ready to play. What do they play?

EVIE: Nothing you'd recognise.

MOBILE: They look very cool.
          A very cool ensemble.

EVIE: Should I open my present, John?

MOBILE: I don't think so.
          You open it and it's over.
          Nothing to look forward to.

EVIE: But then no one
          would ever open anything.

MOBILE: When we met,
          what did we laugh about?

EVIE: What?

MOBILE: When we met, what did we laugh about?

EVIE: John, I don't know. It's sort of long ago.

MOBILE: That rhymed, did you hear, but then it's your
                                        wedding day.
          Things are going to rhyme.

EVIE: You've been sitting there
          some time, haven't you John?

MOBILE: Oh many years.
          Best years of our lives, did you not notice?
          You coughed and they went by. They made you ill.

EVIE: I loved our time together.

MOBILE: Did you love it?
          Take it out on a date. Give it chocolates.
          Put its hand where you want it.

EVIE: I want you always,
         John, to be my friend.

MOBILE: Excellent news.

EVIE: What we had was what we had, and it was special,
         and I'll never forget –

MOBILE: Except what we laughed at.

EVIE: Except what we laughed at, yes. Can I open my present?

MOBILE: You mean *can you open my present
         and then John can you leave.*

EVIE: Be my friend, John,
         it isn't easy for anyone if you're here.

MOBILE: It's easy for me.

EVIE: Then do a thing for me.
         Do it out of pity.

MOBILE: Out of pity?
         On the day of days?

EVIE: Not pity, do it out of
         selflessness. Why are you looking at me?

MOBILE: Why am I looking at you? Selflessness.
         I am leaving my self.

EVIE: That's a start, can your self leave too?
         Only a joke.

MOBILE: I was catching your eye again.
         I was catching it like the old days but unlike
         the old days it will not catch mine at all.

EVIE: I'm looking at you, John. Out of love.

MOBILE: Far out of love.

EVIE: I don't mean out of love,
         I mean, *from* love.

MOBILE: Very, very far from love.

EVIE: You twist and twist. I'm trying to reach, can you see?
         It's my wedding day. *This* is all I am.
         I tried to be a person who was good,
         who never hurt a soul.

MOBILE: Oh I tried that.

EVIE: He is who I chose.
             He is who I picked.

MOBILE: Whom I picked.

EVIE: Go home, John, go home.

MOBILE: What about your present?

EVIE: Will you go if I open this?

MOBILE: I'll go if you open it.

EVIE: Go straight away?

MOBILE: Quick as a flash. Smile.

             (*MOBILE uses his cell phone to take a picture of EVIE.*)

             You didn't smile. Smile this time.

EVIE: And you'll go.

MOBILE: Smile.

             (*She does, he takes another picture. He gives her the gift and
             looks at the picture he took.*)

EVIE: Thank you John.

MOBILE: Like the crocodile.

From

VIGILS
by Noah Haidle

Vigils *was first performed in October 2006 at the*
Goodman Theatre, Chicago.

A fireman died trying to save a baby in a burning house and as
his SOUL left his body his WIDOW caught it and locked it away
in a box. Two years later and she's still clinging to his SOUL and
won't let it go. However, she starts to be wooed by one of her
husband's ex-colleagues and so is forced to think about moving
her life forward. In this scene, the WIDOW prepares for her first
date and rehearses some potential small-talk with the SOUL.

WIDOW/SOUL

WIDOW: It's been two years since you died.

It was fall, like it is now, and the leaves had already fallen. Not that much has changed. I still drink gin and tonic. I still believe happiness never really lasts, I still watch the 'Macy's Thanksgiving Day Parade', and I still love you. I've tried my best not to. I've tried so hard to forget.

SOUL: I know you've tried.

WIDOW: Every day I wake up and think maybe today is the day I won't remember.

And it never is. Every day is the same.

I wear the same black dress. I walk around in the same circles. One of these days I'm going to wear a hole in the floor.

SOUL: Today is different.

WIDOW: Yes, today I'm wearing a brand new purple dress, waiting to be picked up for my first date since you died.

SOUL: Are you nervous?

WIDOW: I told myself I wasn't going to be. But I am.

I don't think I can make small talk anymore.

SOUL: So make big talk.

WIDOW: What's big talk?

SOUL: Ask him if he thinks happiness really lasts.

Ask him if he believes in an afterlife.

Ask him if he thinks each person's soul is judged for the things they do on earth.

WIDOW: Nobody wants to talk about that stuff on a first date. That'll totally freak him out.

SOUL: Fine.

Talk about the weather.

Talk about whatever you like.

WIDOW: Do you think you're going to be judged for what you did on earth?

SOUL: I don't know.

I hope not.

WIDOW: He's here.

(*Calling.*) I'll just be a minute! I just got out of the shower!

Let's practice my small talk.

So, did you catch the game last night?

SOUL: No. I don't have any eyes. I'm a soul.

WIDOW: No. That was small talk.

I'll start over.

So, did you catch the game last night?

SOUL: Yeah.

It sure was a good game.

WIDOW: That's what I thought.

But I think their defense is slipping.

SOUL: I think the best defense is a good offense.

WIDOW: I have to disagree with you.

I think a team with sound defense, while not as flashy as a team with a high-powered offense, is more rooted in the fundamentals of the game and therefore the better team.

SOUL: You make a very good case for the importance of defense.

I change my opinion.

WIDOW: That was pretty good small talk.

Let's try the weather.

You go.

SOUL: So.

Fall sure came early this year, huh?

WIDOW: Sure did.

My husband died in the fall.

So when I see the leaves fall I think of his death.

Even though it's been two years already it seems like only yesterday he was alive and he held me in his arms and we were happy.

(*She starts crying.*)

SOUL: Maybe you should avoid talking about the weather.

WIDOW: You're right.

I'll stick to sports.

SOUL: Or you could talk about the restaurant.

The food.

WIDOW: That's a good idea.

What else do people talk about?

SOUL: Movies. Celebrity gossip. The weather.

WIDOW: But I'm avoiding the weather.

SOUL: Right. You're avoiding the weather.

WIDOW: And I don't go to the movies anymore.

That was something you and I did together and it makes me so sad.

Even the smell of popcorn makes me cry.

SOUL: Celebrity gossip?

WIDOW: I don't know who's a celebrity anymore.

SOUL: Then I guess you should stick to sports.

WIDOW: I'm not ready for this.

SOUL: Yes you are.

Just open the door.

WIDOW: What if I start crying?

SOUL: Say you have to powder your nose.

WIDOW: Powder my nose. Got it.

SOUL: Open the door.

WIDOW: Wish me luck.

SOUL: You don't need luck.

WIDOW: Wish me luck anyway.

SOUL: Good luck.

WIDOW: Thank you.

(*She opens the door.*)

Sorry that took so long.

From

SCENES FROM AN EXECUTION
by Howard Barker

Scenes from an Execution *was first performed at The Almeida
in London in 1990.*

GALACTIA is a female painter living in seventeenth-century
Venice. She has been commissioned to paint a vast canvas to
commemorate Venice's victory at the battle of Lepanto but
decides to portray the true butchery and violence of war rather
than a celebration of the conquest as is usual by painters of
the day. This decision, of course, gets her into trouble with the
Doge, the head of the Venetian state. PRODO is a surviving soldier
from the war; however, he has a crossbow bolt still situated in
his head and his bowel is visible through a gaping battle wound.
Commercially astute, he hires himself out to be gawped at and
GALACTIA invites him to her house so that she can include him
in her picture. However, their meeting challenges him to his
very core.

GALACTIA/PRODO

GALACTIA: Who are you? What do you want?

PRODO: I'm Prodo, the Man with the Crossbow Bolt In His Head.

GALACTIA: Oh, yes.

PRODO: Come at two o'clock, you said.

GALACTIA: Yes…

PRODO: It is two o'clock.

GALACTIA: Yes…

PRODO: I am prompt because I am in demand. Where there is no demand, there is no haste. I would appreciate it if we got on, I am required by a Scotch anatomist at half past three.

GALACTIA: Yes.

PRODO: The fee is seven dollars but no touching. I also have an open wound through which the movement of the bowel may be observed, and my hand is cleft to the wrist, if you're interested. I suggest two dollars for the bowel, and the hand you can look at with my compliments. It is a miracle I am alive, I am a walking manifestation of organic solidarity and the resilience of the Christian state. Shall I proceed?

GALACTIA: Please.

PRODO: I will take off my hat. Are you ready?

GALACTIA: Ready.

(*Pause.*)

PRODO: *Voilà.* The tip is buried in the centre of my brain and yet I suffer no loss of faculties. Pain, yes, and alcohol may occasion blackouts. The shaft may be observed to twitch perceptibly at times of mental exertion. If you would care to set me a simple arithmetical sum I may be able to exhibit this phenomenon.

GALACTIA: Incredible…

PRODO: Go on, ask me.

GALACTIA: Twelve plus five.

PRODO: No, simple, simple.

GALACTIA: Seven times eleven.

PRODO: Seven times eleven…is…

GALACTIA: It's moving…!

PRODO: Is seventy-seven. There is no other recorded evidence of a man sustaining traumatic damage to the brain of this order and retaining consciousness. Would you care to examine the bowel?

GALACTIA: Why not, while we're at it?

PRODO: I do not normally reveal this to a woman.

GALACTIA: Try not to think of me as a woman. Think of me as a painter.

PRODO: I will think of you as a painter. Are you braced for the exposure? I will lower my belt.

GALACTIA: Good God…

PRODO: Please do not faint.

GALACTIA: I am not going to faint…

PRODO: The passage of undigested material along the alimentary canal by the process known as peristalsis can be clearly observed. The retention of the bowel within the pelvic cavity is sometimes problematic given the absence of a significant area of muscularity.

GALACTIA: Spilling your guts…

PRODO: As you wish. That is nine dollars, please.

GALACTIA: Are you bitter, Prodo?

PRODO: Bitter?

GALACTIA: For being left a specimen?

PRODO: God gave me life. God led me to the battle. God steered the bolt, and in his mercy turned my maiming to my benefit. That is nine dollars please.

GALACTIA: Unbuttoning yourself in rich men's rooms…

PRODO: Thank you.

GALACTIA: Grotesque celebrity. Shudder maker. Clinging like a louse to dirty curiosity…

PRODO: Do you require a receipt?

GALACTIA: What about the battle, Prodo?

PRODO: I do not talk about the battle. Thank you. One dollar change.

GALACTIA: Oh, come on, I love your wounds, but tell me how you got them.

PRODO: A treatise on my condition is to be published in the Surgical Gazette. I am also featured on a box of matches, one of which I leave you as a souvenir. I hope you have enjoyed the trivial interest of my misfortune –

GALACTIA: Paint your pain for you.

PRODO: Oh, bloody hell, it's raining –

GALACTIA: Your butchery.

PRODO: Is there a short cut to the Rialto?

GALACTIA: Paint your anger. Paint your grief.

PRODO: I'll see myself out, thank you –

GALACTIA: IDIOT.

(*Pause.*)

PRODO: What?

GALACTIA: Holding your bowel in. With an arrow sticking out the middle of your head. IDIOT.

(*Pause.*)

PRODO: If you'll excuse me, I –

GALACTIA: I am painting the battle, Prodo. Me. The battle which changed you from a man into a monkey. One thousand square feet of canvas. Great empty ground to fill. With noise. Your noise. The noise of men minced. Got to find a new red for all that blood. A red that smells. Don't go, Prodo, holding your bowel in –

PRODO: What sort of woman are you?

GALACTIA: A midwife for your labour. Help you bring the truth to birth. Up there, twice life-size, your half-murder, your half-death. Come on, don't be manly, there's no truth where men are being manly –

PRODO: Don't trust you, got a mad eye –

GALACTIA: Shuffling away there, stop, will you?

PRODO: Afraid of you.

GALACTIA: Afraid of me? Me? Why?

PRODO: Hurt me –

GALACTIA: Never –

PRODO: Ruin it –

GALACTIA: What?

(*Pause.*)

What?

PRODO: MY PEACE WITH LIFE.

GALACTIA: Listen. Listen, look at me, look at me, what sort of a face
do I have? Look at it, is it a good face? Is it generous?

PRODO: It's all right –

GALACTIA: No, it's more than all right, it's a good face, it's an honest
face, broad and generous –

PRODO: Yes –

GALACTIA: Of course it is, I know it is and so do you, I know my
face, I paint it, over and over again, I am not beautiful and I
wouldn't be beautiful if I could be –

PRODO: (*Sarcastically.*) No, you wouldn't be –

GALACTIA: I tell you I would not, I do not trust beauty, it is an
invention and a lie, trust my face, I am a woman who has lived
a little, nothing much, I have not been split up the middle like
you have, but I have picked up a thing or two and I tell you I
have never been at peace with life, I would not be at peace with
life, there is no such thing and those who claim they have it
have drugged their consciences or numbed their pain with futile
repetitions of old catechisms, catechisms like your patter, oh, look
at you. WHO DID IT TO YOU, PRODO, AND WHAT FOR? I
will paint your violence for all the passing crowds who mock your
daft appearance…

(*PRODO sobs.*)

There, there…we must be brave…

PRODO: Nightmares…

GALACTIA: Yes…yes…

PRODO: Down the bottom of the sheets all arms and legs…

GALACTIA: Go on…

PRODO: Bones going…air full of cracking bones…oars going…bones going…

GALACTIA: Yes…

PRODO: Flesh falling down…flesh raining down…bits going… everywhere bits going…rain of bits and THIS TUMULT IN MY BED…!

GALACTIA: Oh, my poor ridiculous man, I shall paint the why of all your terrors, shall I?

PRODO: Give me back my little peace…

GALACTIA: Why was the battle fought, Prodo?

PRODO: My little ease, you –

GALACTIA: Why?

(*Pause.*)

PRODO: Freedom, of course.

GALACTIA: Freedom…

PRODO: Glory, of course.

GALACTIA: Glory…

PRODO: The Honour of the Great Republic and the Humiliation of the Pagan Turk!

GALACTIA: Oh, look, the arrow's twitching! Round and round it goes…

PRODO: DOESN'T!

GALACTIA: Twirling, feathered thing, oh, look!

PRODO: DOESN'T!

GALACTIA: Wonderful man, grappling with dim truths!

PRODO: WHAT ARE YOU TRYING TO DO TO ME, SIGNORA!

(*Pause.*)

GALACTIA: Truth, that's all, just truth. See yourself out, will you?

PRODO: You are an unkind woman, you…

GALACTIA: Thank you for coming.

PRODO: Digging out my –

GALACTIA: Sketchbook! Sketchbook! Where have I –

PRODO: Horror of my –

GALACTIA: Laid it down and –

PRODO: STUPID LIFE.

GALACTIA: Good bye.

From

RAG AND BONE
by Noah Haidle

Rag and Bone *was first performed at the Long Wharf Theatre in New Haven, Connecticut in February 2005.*

Noah Haidle is an American playwright who provides us with a moral tale about the consequences of feeling too much or too little. He uses WB Yeats' poem *The Circus Animals' Desertion* as inspiration: 'Now that my ladder's gone/I must lie down where all the ladders start/In the foul rag and bone shop of the heart'. Jeff and GEORGE own a ladder shop where GEORGE has a black market operation in stolen hearts, secretly selling them to people who can't feel enough emotion in their lives or who want to feel something different. A CUSTOMER enters to survey the merchandise.

GEORGE/CUSTOMER

GEORGE: You say you're looking for a very special ladder.

CUSTOMER: Yes. I hate being on the ground.

(*GEORGE takes out a stethoscope. Listens to her heart.*)

GEORGE: What seems to be the problem?

CUSTOMER: It's like in the movie of my life I'm not the lead.

I don't even have a supporting part.

I'm an extra, a silhouette in the background, out of focus, anonymous.

GEORGE: You've come to the right place.

CUSTOMER: You can make me the lead in the movie of my life?

GEORGE: I'll try my best.

CUSTOMER: I don't even need to be the lead. Just a couple of good, meaty scenes would be enough.

(*GEORGE takes out a cooler. Holds up hearts, one at a time.*)

GEORGE: Here we have a very nice heart. Took it off a paediatrician who loved children more than anything in the world. She used to give free medical care to anyone in need.

This is a nice heart as well. Took it off a public defender who helped all the neediest cases. And even though the system is corrupt she kept with it.

CUSTOMER: What about that one?

GEORGE: I see you have a very good eye.

This is the heart of a poet.

(*He takes out the heart of the POET, which should look pretty much like all the other hearts.*)

Took it off a poet who lived his whole life in pursuit of truth and beauty.

This heart would let you see the world with a profound clarity. You'd see people as they truly are. And would give you a sense of empathy that borders on the clairvoyant. You would feel other people's suffering.

CUSTOMER: How much is it?

GEORGE: Please don't take offence to this. But I don't think you could handle the heart of a poet.

CUSTOMER: I used to write poetry.

In college.

GEORGE: Please. Let's move on.

CUSTOMER: Fine.

Tell me more about the public defender.

GEORGE: You'll feel lots of things with this heart.

Empathy. Passion. Mercy.

This is a very, very good heart.

CUSTOMER: But it's not the heart of a poet.

GEORGE: No.

CUSTOMER: Will you be getting any minor poets?

Something I could handle.

GEORGE: I can never predict my inventory. I may get one tomorrow. I may not get one for ten years.

CUSTOMER: Tell me about the paediatrician.

GEORGE: Mostly you would feel an enormous sense of compassion. And deserved righteousness.

CUSTOMER: What's that other one?

The one in the back.

GEORGE: That's not for sale.

CUSTOMER: Why not?

Is it the heart of Mother Theresa or something?

GEORGE: It's my mother's heart.

CUSTOMER: Oh.

I'm sorry.

GEORGE: Not your fault.

CUSTOMER: So my choices are between the paediatrician and the public defender?

GEORGE: That's right.

CUSTOMER: I guess I'll take the public defender.

GEORGE: Excellent choice. Have you eaten anything in the past twenty-four hours?

(*She takes out an American Express card.*)

CUSTOMER: No, you're not supposed to eat anything twenty-four hours before major surgery.

GEORGE: That's right.

(*He takes out a hand-held credit card swiper.*)

In case you're worried about appearances, the receipt will simply read 'The Ladder Store'.

(*He swipes her card. Gives it back to her.*)

CUSTOMER: Could I just try the poet's heart? Just to feel what it's like?

GEORGE: I'm afraid that's impossible.

CUSTOMER: Just for a second. I'll pay extra. Please.

(*He takes her card and swipes it again.*)

GEORGE: Fine.

But only for a little while.

From

ROOM TO LET
by Paul Tucker

Room to Let *was first performed at the Chelsea Centre Theatre, London, in May 1999.*

JANET is forty-eight years old and has lived with her partner, EDDIE, for twenty-four years. EDDIE is fifty-three years old and unemployed after being made redundant over seven years ago. He sees himself as 'a bit thick, bit slow' which he puts down to being kicked in the head by a horse. He isn't JANET's ideal man and she spends a great deal of time abusing him. Despite this, she still wants to marry him as she's always wanted to be married. She has decided to rent out the spare room so that there will be enough money for the wedding and a honeymoon at Butlins in Bognor. Unfortunately EDDIE isn't keen and, later on in the play, we learn that he's already married but walked out on his wife and child many years ago.

In this scene, we find EDDIE watching television. However, as soon as he hears JANET return home from work he turns the television off.

EDDIE/JANET

(*JANET goes over to the TV and feels the back of the TV set. It is warm. She takes off her shoe, goes over to EDDIE and hits him with it. She knows how to use it. EDDIE absorbs the attack.*)

JANET: What 'ave I told yer about watching telly in the day? (*She stops hitting him and points.*) Shopping.

(*EDDIE takes the bags into the kitchen and starts to unpack. JANET watches him with her arms folded.*)

Put it in, don't throw it in.

EDDIE: Stop watching me then.

JANET: I have to watch yer, make sure you do a proper job.

(*He continues putting the food away. EDDIE holds up a packet of something.*)

Cupboard.

(*He puts it in the cupboard. He holds up something else.*)

Fridge… (*Something else.*) Fridge… Freezer.

(*He puts the shopping in the fridge. JANET changes her standing position so that she can see him put things in the fridge. He takes out a family bag of crisps.*)

EDDIE: Why do you always have to get these ones?

JANET: Why? What's up with 'em?

EDDIE: They're crap. They stick in yer throat.

JANET: They're good enough for you.

EDDIE: They always put too much salt in 'em.

JANET: Now listen here monkey-man, I buy you sodding good food so don't start arguing with me.

EDDIE: You have 'em then.

JANET: (*Proud.*) I shall have 'em. I shall have 'em on bread.

(*JANET takes off her coat and hangs it up. EDDIE finishes the unpacking and sits back down, picks up the paper so he doesn't have to look at her or speak to her. JANET sits down on the sofa ready for her second attack.*)

I suppose you aint been out today either. (*EDDIE shakes head.*) It's a good job I go out int it, go out to work so we can get some money in. I sweat cobs for you.

EDDIE: (*Prodding himself with thumb.*) I spent twelve years in the hosiery industry missus, so don't go round telling me about going out.

JANET: Phhh! Twelve years! Twelve days more like.

EDDIE: I've told yer, I daren't go out cause someone keeps following me.

JANET: Follow yer! Who wants to follow you? The only thing that follows you, is yer own bad smell.

EDDIE: Listen pal, I know when someone's following me, alright?

JANET: Well you could do something for me then, do some house work. You needn't pull that face either – go out and get a job.

EDDIE: (*Tiresome.*) I…don't…want…a…job.

JANET: Yes you do! It aint right for a man to sit in the house all day.

EDDIE: It aint right for a man to work all day.

JANET: (*Tuts, shakes head in disgust.*) People have to go out to work to get money. So they can live, so they can afford holidays or go pickernicking in the country.

EDDIE: I don't wanna go on picnics.

JANET: Well I do! I wanna go out now and again! I've been stuck in this house for the last twenty-four years! (*Gets out Argos catalogue from handbag, puts it on table*.) I've bought that for yer as well.

EDDIE: What do I want that for?

JANET: So you can get me an engagement ring. (*Gets out Butlins holiday brochure.*) And I've got yer that so yer can take me on our honeymoon.

EDDIE: (*Pulls head back.*) Aww you aint still going on about bloody marriage are yer?

JANET: Listen, I've been waiting half my bloody life for a ring on this finger.

EDDIE: Look, what's the point in getting married when we've been living together all these bleeding years?

JANET: (*Shaking fist.*) Cause…it…shows…me…how…much…you… love… ME.

EDDIE: Aww Christ.

JANET: You don't wanna marry me do yer?

EDDIE: Aww God forbid me.

JANET: You don't love me do yer?

EDDIE: I do!

JANET: Well what yer scared of then? Have you got another wife or something?

EDDIE: No!

JANET: Well you can take me up that bloody aisle then. I aint waiting any longer. I want a July wedding. And then we're going to Butlins for our honeymoon. Are you listening?

EDDIE: (*Reading paper.*) Yeah.

JANET: Well you could show a bit more excitement then!

EDDIE: What?

JANET: Oh forget it, I mind's well talk to meself. Be a lot more interesting. God, if I knew my life would end up like this when I was a teenager, I would have drowned meself.

EDDIE: If I knew my life would end up like this, I would have done it for yer.

JANET: (*Nodding.*) I'll remember that when you wanna borrow some money.

EDDIE: Listen, listen to me luv. We haven't got no money to get married. It's sodding expensive these days.

JANET: That's why we're getting a lodger in! I keep telling yer! If we charge thirty quid a week for that room, we'll have saved more than enough in a couple of months. That reminds me, has anyone bin?

EDDIE: Look luv, let's just take one thing at a time. You can't be hasty with these things – we might end up with one of those axe murderers or something.

JANET: Aww shurrup yer daft sod. You're just scared of having a real man around. Yes you are! You're scared to see what real men are like instead of farting and belching round the house all day.

(*JANET kicks off her shoes. She rubs her feet. Sweat has come through the toe bits in her tights. She takes off her tights, holds them out to EDDIE.*)

Here, you can hang these up an all. Give 'em a good airing.

(*EDDIE sighs, gets up, hangs the American tan tights near the window. JANET takes the tub of margarine off the table, scoops some out and rubs marg into her feet. EDDIE resumes his paper-reading. She clearly enjoys rubbing in the marg, pursing her lips, giving out slow huffs and puffs and pulling faces of 'what a day.'*)

Aww me tootsies ache they do. I've been on 'em all day. Joyce at work, her husband rubs her feet for her. She doesn't have to ask him to rub her toes. He rubs crème fraiche into 'em. You wunt do that for me!

(*EDDIE sighs, rolls his eyes back. As she starts on the other foot, she finds a piece of paper screwed up between the cushions. She unwraps it. EDDIE hides behind his newspaper. She reads it.*)

Oi! What the hell's this?

EDDIE: (*Playing dumb.*) What?

JANET: You know what! (*Reads it.*) 'Came to look at room this afternoon… Knocking for ages… Could hear racing on television…but nobody came to the door…will return this evening…thank you kind sirs…bye…' How long 'as this been here?

EDDIE: Dunno what yer talking about.

JANET: (*Pushing bottom set of teeth out.*) How… LONG…has this been here?

EDDIE: I'm not sure.

JANET: HOW LONG?

EDDIE: Since today!

JANET: Well why dint you let the bleeder in and show him the room?

EDDIE: Cause I don't wanna get married and I don't want a bleeding lodger!

(*JANET quickly scoops off the excess marg off her foot and wipes it back into the tub. She storms over to EDDIE. EDDIE lifts his arm up to protect himself.*)

JANET: (*Grabs his ear.*) Listen here pally – we're getting a lodger and then you're taking me up the 'kin aisle!

The Books

THE MURDERS AT ARGOS, CRESSIDA AMONG THE GREEKS
by David Foley

ISBN 978-1-84002-323-7

INSIDE OUT
by Tanika Gupta

ISBN 978-1-84002-352-7

BLACK CROWS
by Linda Brogan

ISBN 978-1-84002-737-2

MERCY FINE
by Shelley Silas

ISBN 978-1-84002-637-5

A BRIEF HISTORY OF HELEN OF TROY
by Mark Schultz

ISBN 978-1-84002-634-4

CATCH
by de Angelis, Gupta, Feehily, Moss and Wade

ISBN 978-1-84002-716-7

STEALING SWEETS AND PUNCHING PEOPLE
by Phil Porter

ISBN 978-1-84002-404-3

GET UP AND TIE YOUR FINGERS
by Ann Coburn
from *Three Plays*

ISBN 978-1-84002-364-0

FALLING
by Shelley Silas

ISBN 978-1-84002-328-2

CONCEALMENT
by Reza de Wet
from *Two Plays*

ISBN 978-1-84002-492-0

MAD MARGARET'S REVENGE
by Lesley Ross

from *The Jolly Folly of Polly, the Scottish Trolley Dolly*

ISBN 978-1-84002-541-5

HARVEST
by Richard Bean

ISBN 978-1-84002-594-1

THE BOGUS WOMAN
by Kay Adshead

ISBN 978-1-84002-209-4

WHO'S BREAKING
by Philip Osment

from *Plays for Young People*

ISBN 978-1-84002-272-8

CALCUTTA KOSHER
by Shelley Silas

ISBN 978-1-84002-430-2

MONSTER
by Duncan Macmillan

ISBN 978-1-84002-759-4

CROSSFIRE
by Michel Azama, translated by Nigel Gearing

ISBN 978-1-870259-34-7

CAR
by Chris O'Connell

from *Street Trilogy*

ISBN 978-1-84002-389-3

TALKIN' LOUD
by Trevor Williams

ISBN 978-1-84002-472-2

BURNING BLUE
by DMW Greer

ISBN 978-1-84002-024-3

PLAYING FIELDS
by Neela Dolezalova

ISBN 978-1-84002-349-7

INCARCERATOR
by Torben Betts

from *Plays Two*

ISBN 978-1-84002-200-1

THE WAR NEXT DOOR
by Tamsin Oglesby
ISBN 978-1-84002-729-7

DEADEYE
by Amber Lone
ISBN 978-1-84002-707-5

FIVE VISIONS OF THE FAITHFUL
by Torben Betts
from *Plays Two*
ISBN 978-1-84002-200-1

EVERY BREATH
by Judith Johnson
ISBN 978-1-84002-668-9

THE POSSIBILITIES: REASONS FOR THE FALL OF EMPERORS
by Howard Barker
from *Plays One*
ISBN 978-1-84002-612-2

TENDER
by Abi Morgan
ISBN 978-1-84002-238-4

PROVING MR JENNINGS
by James Walker
ISBN 978-1-84002-719-8

SCENES FROM THE BACK OF BEYOND
by Meredith Oakes
ISBN 978-1-84002-708-2

THE LAST CONFESSION
by Roger Crane
ISBN 978-1-84002-779-2

BREATHING CORPSES
by Laura Wade
ISBN 978-1-84002-546-0

VIRGINS
by John Retallack
from *Company of Angels*
ISBN 978-1-84002-725-9

OTHER HANDS
by Laura Wade
ISBN 978-1-84002-650-4

OFF CAMERA
by Marcia Layne
ISBN 978-1-84002-381-7

SILENCE AND VIOLENCE
by Torben Betts
from *Plays Two*
ISBN 978-1-84002-200-1

THINGS YOU SHOULDN'T SAY PAST MIDNIGHT
by Peter Ackerman
ISBN 978-1-84002-354-1

THE FOREVER WALTZ
by Glyn Maxwell
ISBN 978-1-84002-591-0

A MATTER OF LIFE AND DEATH
adapted by Tom Morris and Emma Rice
ISBN 978-1-84002-781-5

**VIGILS
RAG AND BONE**
by Noah Haidle
from *Three Plays*
ISBN 978-1-84002-750-1

CAMILLE
adapted by Neil Bartlett from *La Dame aux camélias* by Alexandre Dumas *fils*
ISBN 978-1-84002-360-2

SCENES FROM AN EXECUTION
by Howard Barker
from *Plays One*
ISBN 978-1-84002-612-2

UNDER THE BLACK FLAG
by Simon Bent
ISBN 978-1-84002-671-9

ROOM TO LET
by Paul Tucker
ISBN 978-1-84002-125-7

LOVE SONG
by John Kolvenbach
ISBN 978-1-84002-715-0